# How to Read Your Child Like a Book

by
**Dr. Lynn Weiss**

D1231145

**Meadowbrook Press**
Distributed by Simon & Schuster
New York

Library of Congress Cataloging-in-Publication Data

Weiss, Lynn.
    How to read your child like a book / Lynn Weiss.
        p. cm.
    ISBN 0-88166-281-X (Meadowbrook)
    ISBN 0-671-52124-1 (Simon & Schuster)
    1. Child development. 2. Child psychology. 3. Child rearing.
    I. Title.
    HQ772.W364   1997
    305.231—dc21                                                97-10582
                                                                    CIP

Editor: Liya Lev Oertel
Proofreader: Nancy Baldrica
Production Manager: Joe Gagne
Production Assistant: Danielle White
Text Design: Amy Unger
Cover Design: Maclean & Tuminelly

Published by Meadowbrook Press, 5451 Smetana Drive, Minnetonka, Minnesota 55343

BOOK TRADE DISTRIBUTION by Simon & Schuster, a division of Simon and Schuster, Inc., 1230 Avenue of the Americas, New York, NY 10020

00 99 98 97   10 9 8 7 6 5 4 3 2 1

Printed in the United States of America

## Dedication

To all children and parents—past, present, and future

## Acknowledgements

Twenty-five years ago I was privileged to work with many teachers and young children in the Dallas/Ft. Worth, Texas, child-care area. One teacher stands out in my mind: Mae Burton. From observing the way she worked with children, I began to appreciate the wonderful emotional and behavioral resources within young children. She taught me how to assist children and parents to make the most of innate drives and capabilities. Thanks to Mae Burton.

I also give thanks to my sons, Aaron and Mendel Weiss, who shared their growing up with me. We learned together how to meet their needs in the most satisfactory way possible for each of us. I've been truly blessed to be their parent.

Thanks to those who helped me write this book:

To my agent, Mary Kelly.

To Janis Dworkis and Liya Lev Oertel who provided editorial assistance.

To Mary Schultz, the Comma Queen, who supported me and took charge of seeing that many errant commas were put in their place.

And, special thanks to all the parents and children of the world to whom this book is dedicated.

# CONTENTS

**Introduction** . . . . . . . . . . . . . . . . . . . . . . . . . . . . . . . . . . . . . . . .vii

STAGE 1: **TRUST** (BIRTH TO EIGHTEEN MONTHS) . . . . . . . . . . . . . . 1
    Crying . . . . . . . . . . . . . . . . . . . . . . . . . . . . . . . . . . . 3
    Acting Irritably . . . . . . . . . . . . . . . . . . . . . . . . . . . 7
    Needing a Lot of Help . . . . . . . . . . . . . . . . . . . 11
    Showing Fear . . . . . . . . . . . . . . . . . . . . . . . . . . 17
    Appearing Lethargic . . . . . . . . . . . . . . . . . . . . 21
    Being "Too Good" . . . . . . . . . . . . . . . . . . . . . . 25

STAGE 2: **IDENTITY** (EIGHTEEN MONTHS TO THREE YEARS) . . . . 31
    Experiencing Separation Anxiety . . . . . . . . . . 32
    Moving Away from You . . . . . . . . . . . . . . . . . 37
    Being Self-Centered and Possessive . . . . . . . . . 42
    Discovering the Body . . . . . . . . . . . . . . . . . . . . 52
    Doing Things without Help . . . . . . . . . . . . . . . 56
    Having Feelings . . . . . . . . . . . . . . . . . . . . . . . . 61
    Making Things Happen . . . . . . . . . . . . . . . . . . 66
    Opposing You . . . . . . . . . . . . . . . . . . . . . . . . . . 71
    Behaving Aggressively . . . . . . . . . . . . . . . . . . . 76
    Being Stubborn . . . . . . . . . . . . . . . . . . . . . . . . 81

STAGE 3: **COMPETENCE** (THREE TO FOUR YEARS) . . . . . . . . . . 87
    Exploring . . . . . . . . . . . . . . . . . . . . . . . . . . . . . 89
    Experimenting . . . . . . . . . . . . . . . . . . . . . . . . . 93
    Wanting to Help . . . . . . . . . . . . . . . . . . . . . . . 97
    Expanding Interests . . . . . . . . . . . . . . . . . . . . 101
    "Misbehaving" . . . . . . . . . . . . . . . . . . . . . . . . 105
    Feeling Fearful . . . . . . . . . . . . . . . . . . . . . . . . 109
    Feeling Overwhelmed and Frustrated . . . . . . 114
    Distinguishing Fantasy and Reality . . . . . . . . 119

CONTENTS

STAGE 4: **POWER** (FOUR TO FIVE AND A HALF YEARS) . . . . . . . . 123

Discovering Power . . . . . . . . . . . . . . . . . . . . . 125
Taking Power . . . . . . . . . . . . . . . . . . . . . . . . 129
Building Power . . . . . . . . . . . . . . . . . . . . . . . 134
Testing Power . . . . . . . . . . . . . . . . . . . . . . . 140
Pushing Your Limits . . . . . . . . . . . . . . . . . . . 144
Exploring . . . . . . . . . . . . . . . . . . . . . . . . . . 150
Protecting Himself . . . . . . . . . . . . . . . . . . . . 155
Losing Power . . . . . . . . . . . . . . . . . . . . . . . . 159
Expressing Power Emotionally . . . . . . . . . . . 164

STAGE 5: **SELF-CONTROL** (FIVE TO SIX AND A HALF YEARS) . . . 169

Establishing Control . . . . . . . . . . . . . . . . . . . 171
Feeling Empathy . . . . . . . . . . . . . . . . . . . . . . 176
Developing Honesty . . . . . . . . . . . . . . . . . . . 181
Requiring Fairness . . . . . . . . . . . . . . . . . . . . 186
Handling Differences . . . . . . . . . . . . . . . . . . 191
Being Self-Controlled . . . . . . . . . . . . . . . . . . 196
Behaving "Too Good" . . . . . . . . . . . . . . . . . . 201
Experimenting . . . . . . . . . . . . . . . . . . . . . . . 206

**Parting Remarks** . . . . . . . . . . . . . . . . . . . . . . . . . . . . . . . . . . . 211

**Assessment Checklist for Preschoolers** . . . . . . . . . . . . . . . . . 212

# Introduction

The job of raising your child is likely to be the most exciting, scary challenge you will ever attempt. Generations of influences and experiences affect child rearing. Just as your child is affected by you, so were you affected by your parents, who were affected by your grandparents. And many others—relatives, family friends, child-care workers, and teachers—share responsibility. But none of them has as much influence on your child's growth process as you.

Your child brings into the world a unique set of characteristics. Activity level, disposition, potential for intellectual and physical development, creativity, and style of neurobiochemical wiring all contribute to the mix. In addition, an intense interaction between your child and you, and between your child and other caregivers, takes place from the very beginning. Each interaction leaves its mark on your child.

If you were to grow a plant from seed, with the hope that it would mature into a healthy, flowering shrub, you would learn what the plant needs. You would care for it tenderly, water it, feed it, and shelter it from abusive elements. You would prune and guide the plant according to its particular needs. You would not yank its branches or shake it roughly. You would neither neglect it nor overfeed it. After receiving your special care early in its life, the seedling would eventually grow into a strong, mature tree, able to withstand stress and strain.

Your child needs the same kind of care and guidance, especially during the preschool years, and suffers from the lack of either.

This book will provide you with the information you need to build a successful partnership between you and your child. During the first six years of a child's life, each child will pass through five developmental stages—trust, identity, competence, power, and self-control. Your understanding of these stages will give you the tools to help your child become an emotionally healthy, happy, responsible person. Each stage augments, in a logical, understandable sequence, the previous stage. If your child moves through the experiences and demands of these early years successfully, he or she will have a solid emotional foundation upon which to structure all later life. A child who doesn't build an early foundation will struggle throughout life to achieve the missing stages.

As a parent who cares about your child's growth, you strive to achieve the goals set by each developmental stage. You might bump up against difficulties that result from your own limitations in each of these five areas. A lack of understanding of these developmental stages has blocked parents of all generations from fully helping their offspring to grow completely. But if you understand the stages that make up your child's growth, provide support for your child's needs, and look at the world through your child's eyes, you can give your child the best possible chance for success in life.

# Birth to Eighteen Months:
## Trust

 From birth to eighteen months, your baby depends on you to understand his needs, so he can grow to become a trusting person. Through experience, your baby learns to trust that his basic needs will be met. In this section you will learn how to help your baby develop a strong foundation of trust that will remain with him for the rest of his life.

Because your baby's communication skills are limited, you will have to interpret his crying and behavior to understand his needs. This section covers the following observable behaviors: crying, acting irritably, needing a lot of help, showing fear, appearing lethargic, and being too good.

• Crying announces that your baby is hungry, wet, or physically uncomfortable. Your baby will also cry to let you know that he feels pain or wants to be touched. Your response will help him learn to trust that others will be there for him.

• When your baby is irritable, fussy, or impatient, you know that he needs help. Since he cannot yet take care of himself, your baby must know that you will not let these irritations continue without trying to help him. By trusting in your help, he'll develop an optimistic, hopeful attitude toward life.

• When your baby needs a lot of help or is afraid of something, sometimes all you can do is be present, even though you can't fix what is troubling him. Your baby depends on you to soothe, understand, and protect him. Although he can't quite understand what is happening, he knows when you are with him, and trust develops from your staying with him.

• Your baby will appear lethargic when he needs more stimulation or when he believes that his basic needs won't be met. His sense of trust will be limited as a result.

• Finally, you will learn the guidelines for dealing with the "good" child who doesn't naturally make demands to get what he needs. Although this child is easy to live with, his development of trust can be compromised due to his lack of assertiveness. A "good" child needs you teach him to be expressive, so he can ensure that his needs will be met.

Helping your child build trust is very important—the trust your child gains now will shape the way in which he will perceive the world for the rest of his life.

# Crying

## Your Child's Behavior

When you first brought your new baby home from the hospital, her crying made you feel tense. You weren't sure what she needed or why she was crying. But as you and your baby got to know each other, you began to recognize that she used different cries to communicate her needs. You learned which cry meant she was hungry. And you began to feel more confident, because when you heard that cry, you knew how to soothe her.

Now that your child is a bit older, sometimes she may seem to cry just because she needs attention. When you pick her up and cuddle her, she may stop crying. You've also heard cries that let you know when your baby is sick. You may not always be able to soothe a sick child with just a cuddle—and that may make you feel helpless. But when that happens, you've learned to take your baby to the doctor. And when you follow the doctor's directions, your baby usually feels better.

When you can meet your baby's needs—when you can soothe her tears away—you feel great. You like the wonderful feeling of helping her feel good. Sometimes, however, you can't figure out why she is crying or what you can do to soothe her. And when you can't figure out what is bothering her, you feel helpless.

## What Your Child May Be Thinking or Feeling

I'm just beginning to figure things out. One of the things I do know is how to get Mommy or Daddy to help me when I need them; I cry.

At first, crying just came out of me and I didn't know why. But now I can use it to get their attention. When I didn't feel well and I cried, Mommy tried to help me. But nothing she did made me feel better. Then she took me to the doctor, and I started to feel better.

Sometimes I cry when I get lonely or afraid—when I'm all alone and I can't see Mommy or Daddy. When I cry, they move me closer to them so I can see them. Or they hold me. And then I feel better because I know someone is around who can help me get what I need. I can trust them to take care of me.

If I feel wet or sticky and I cry out, Mommy or Daddy comes to make me feel better. They take the wetness away, wipe me off, and pat me dry. Then I see a big can that sprinkles powder on me. I love the powder! After they put a new soft diaper on me, they talk to me in sweet sounds. I've learned to trust that this will happen every time I cry.

## What It Means

Your child communicates by crying when she needs something. At first, you don't know what that something is—neither does she. But together you will establish a communication system that, in most cases, guides you. You will be able to figure out how to help her. How wonderful!

The basic needs of infancy are fairly simple. Your baby requires food when she is hungry. She needs physical comfort when she is uncomfortable, which means being dry, neither too hot nor too cold, and pain-free. And she needs to be touched and loved.

If you think about what infancy feels like, one word comes to mind: helplessness. Interestingly, that helplessness serves a special purpose in the development of your child. It teaches your child to trust others to meet the needs she cannot meet herself.

Trust is the first developmental stage your child experiences: trust that her needs will be met from outside herself. Your child needs what she needs when she needs it. But she cannot yet take care of herself. She is dependent upon you and other adults or older children to help her.

From a starting point of profound helplessness as a young infant, your child spends her first eighteen months growing physically, cognitively, emotionally, and socially. During this time, your child's main job is to learn trust—trust that others will help her when she needs help.

Parents try to meet their child's needs, yet sometimes, inadvertently, those needs may not be met. Maybe you become ill, and your child experiences many caregivers—each with a different routine, feel, and sound. As a result, your child's trust may not develop as smoothly as it would had you consistently cared for her. Or maybe you are anxious and, since young children are emotional sponges, your child absorbs your anxiety and feels hurt by it. You wouldn't mean harm, but your child would get hurt nonetheless. Or, perhaps you decide to teach your child patience at this age. Your efforts would undercut the development of a strong sense of trust.

At the beginning of infancy, all of your child's expressions of need must be met as soon as possible. From your infant's perspective, a minute feels like an hour. But as your child gains experience during her first year and a half, she learns your routines. After she cries out of hunger several times, she learns that you respond by saying something reassuring and bringing her food. Eventually your child begins to recognize sequences of events. If she's bottle-fed, she'll even recognize the sound of the refrigerator door opening; even though your child doesn't know what the sound is, she will learn to associate it with food. Soon, just the sound of the refrigerator door opening begins to comfort her.

When your child is sick, your presence provides her with comfort, even when you can't help her directly. And she'll learn that, at least, you don't abandon her.

Your child will also learn that the people you bring to help her are safe, and that they will also help her. You are the crucial key to your child's development of trust. Even children who are in day care most of their waking hours develop their primary trust from their parents. From the bond between you and your child comes fulfillment of her most basic of human needs, and so she learns to trust. From that trust, your child learns to feel safe and secure and, later, to develop intimate relationships. Patience, honesty, and the ability to empathize are also offshoots of trust. And finally, your child experiences a joyfulness of spirit and the ability to play. All this comes from developing trust during infancy.

## What to Do

**Be attentive and fulfill your child's needs quickly.**
Time is of the essence in infancy. Let no need go unmet for any length of time. Interpret crying as a communication that your baby needs something, and try a variety of things to meet that need, all

the time speaking softly and comfortingly to your child, so that she senses you are trying.

**Be consistent.**
Consistency is crucial during infancy. Routines—regular caregivers and familiar environments, foods, and even clothing—help your child learn the patterns upon which trust is built. If someone must take over for you, tell that person how you do things so he or she can imitate you. If your life changes, try to keep your child's routines as regular as possible.

**Provide your child with touch and attention.**
Besides food and bodily comfort, your child needs to feel and hear you. Hold your child during feeding. This is crucial; no propped bottles, please.

Take your child into the room where you are working, so she can see and hear you. This will contribute to her bonding with you. Remember, this contact is a link that builds trust.

## What Not to Do

**Do not try to teach your infant patience.**
Infancy is not the time to teach your child to wait. In fact, a child whose needs have been met develops a sense of trust and, automatically, develops patience as an offshoot. Let patience develop naturally.

**Do not become impatient if you can't comfort your child.**
Although you are likely to feel frustrated when you can't figure out what your child needs, know that in the process of trying, some communication is taking place. Feeling impatient, either with yourself or your infant, when you can't comfort her is natural, but instead of letting your impatience build, get help. Call a friend, family member, or doctor's office, and get help for yourself and your child.

**Do not believe that you have to be a perfect parent.**
Children are very resilient; you don't have to do everything perfectly to help them develop a sense of trust. In fact, you have to mess up a lot to inhibit the development of trust and bonding. Relax, enjoy your child, and let her know that you enjoy her.

# Acting Irritably

## Your Child's Behavior

Sometimes, your baby may act irritably. He may fuss, cry, and squirm when you try to hold him.

When your baby was much younger, he may have been able to wait more patiently to be fed or picked up. But now, if you don't pick him up right away, he may fuss. When you try to feed him, he may spit the food out or take it with his hands and drop it on the floor.

If someone other than you wants to hold him, your baby may push away and almost try to jump back into your arms. And if he does let anyone else hold him, he may seem comfortable for only a few minutes before wanting to come back to you.

When your baby acts this way in public, you may feel embarrassed. And you may wonder what happened to your sweet, placid little baby who just wanted to be fed or held—and who seemed to trust anyone to do that.

## What Your Child May Be Thinking or Feeling

Too much is going on inside and outside of me these days. Something sharp is poking me in my mouth and it hurts. My body doesn't feel very good. I don't want to be still. I don't like being in the same place all the time. I want to move around. I can turn myself over, but I can't always move myself forward or backward if I want to.

I'm tired of feeling so helpless, but I can't seem to do much about getting what I need. It seems as though everything takes too long: my food, my bath, my car ride.

Mommy is my special person, and I want to be with her or Daddy. I don't want to be with anyone else. I trust Mommy and Daddy, and I can't trust anyone else the same way.

But even Mommy and Daddy aren't happy with me all the time. Today I discovered that if I drop a cracker on the floor, Mommy will pick it up. But when I tried to do it again, she talked to me in a loud, unhappy voice, and she said, "No." I don't know what that means, but it didn't make me feel good.

I'm not very happy right now. I just feel bad.

## What It Means

By the time your child is six to seven months old, he can tell the difference between you and a stranger. By the time he reaches eleven months, he probably doesn't want anything to do with strangers. He wants you—all the time. You are likely to feel as if he'd like you to hold him twenty-four hours a day.

You must also realize that, although your mother or relatives are very familiar to you, they are no different than any other stranger to your child. So when your child pulls away from Grandma and Grandpa, encourage them to realize that his behavior is normal and natural. He simply hasn't learned to trust these strange people yet.

In all probability, your child is also teething during this time, which means his whole mouth, face, and throat are irritated. That is not a good feeling. In addition, your child has been doing a lot of new growing, and his whole body probably feels a little stretched and stressed.

All this change affects the trust that your child has built to date. Such a threat to his security naturally makes him feel fussy, restless, and impatient in situations that didn't bother him before.

Your child is not the totally helpless baby he used to be, but he's not yet very mobile. He's crawling and trying to walk. But he falls a lot. It scares him. Falling while starting to do new things hurts your child's body and pride, which makes him feel irritable. Your child needs extra encouragement and help from you so he doesn't lose trust in himself and his abilities. Remember, your child doesn't realize what is going on and, as a result, may experience a loss of trust unless you are there to help, rescue, and generally soothe and shield him from hurt.

Your child is probably also beginning to play with his food and is getting into trouble because of it, which is a new thing for him. He didn't get into trouble as an infant, and he's not too sure he likes it.

Your child doesn't really understand what he does wrong or why people are grouchy with him. He doesn't even really know what "no" means, but he can tell it isn't good. That makes him anxious. Your child doesn't feel as safe as he used to. All this change challenges your child's ability to trust.

Your job during this period is to help your child retain the trust that his needs will be met while he changes and grows. Some of the things your child does will require you to set limits. You must guide your child along the path between what he can and can't do.

Because of the stresses your child is experiencing, he is less easy to comfort than he used to be. And sometimes what you expect from your child will cause him to be distressed. So, although in the long run your child needs your limits to feel safe, don't apply those limits harshly. Just be firm.

Physically, emotionally, and socially, your baby is growing up. He's changing right in front of your eyes. And you must help your child change in a way that doesn't scare him or irritate you too much. Throughout, your child's trust must remain intact.

## What to Do

### Realize your child is still a baby.
Even though your child is no longer an infant, you must realize that he is still a baby. He is trying new things and reacting differently than before, but he is still very, very dependent upon you. Use sensitivity to help your child change and explore.

### Distract your child when he does something you don't like.
If your child drops a cracker on the floor or pulls at your earring, simply distract him from the undesired activity. Direct your child's attention to something else, and remove the object from his reach so he is not tempted to play with it further.

### Soothe your child when he fusses.
Instead of always trying to fix every thing that upsets your child at this stage, you may find that simply noting how he feels is soothing for him. You may say, "I'm sorry you feel irritable today. You'll feel better later." Don't make a big deal of your child's moods and fussing. But do acknowledge that they are distressful to him. This acknowledgment lets your child know you understand.

Realize that your child's irritability and fussiness are only the result of the many things that affect him. Remember, most of these irritations are temporary and will pass. Let your child know that everyone has times like this. Although your child won't completely understand what you're talking about, he'll get an idea of what you're trying to say. That will help you bond together and will increase your child's trust.

**Understand that your child learns by "misbehaving."**
Many times your infant will seem to be "getting into things," but he is really just exploring and trying to figure out his world. If you get irritable with your child for this type of exploration, you damage the trust you've already helped him develop. Although he may seem to be having "fun," your child is not trying to irritate you.

## What Not to Do

**Do not punish or discipline your child at this age.**
Your child doesn't know that what he is doing is wrong; he is exploring and learning a lot about the things in his world. He doesn't mean to do wrong. Your child just does what comes naturally.

**Do not push your child to go to relatives or friends.**
Even though another adult's feelings may get hurt, never force or even push your child to go to another adult until he is ready. Let your child learn to trust the other person before he makes his move.

If the adult acts hurt or offended, simply say, "I'm sorry you're feeling hurt, but he will come to you when he is ready. It's not you. He is simply hesitant at this age."

**Do not feel you have done something wrong if your child is fussy.**
You may find it difficult to remain objective when your child is fussy. You are likely to feel as though you have done something wrong, or that you ought to be able to fix the situation. But much of what bothers your child may be beyond your control.

Think about what you have done or failed to do that might have created your child's fussiness, and if you don't find anything, relax. Don't blame yourself. But remember to soothe your child, because he also doesn't understand why he feels bad. Above all, don't get angry at your child or reject him.

# Needing a Lot of Help

## Your Child's Behavior

Your baby may start a pattern of crying every day at the same time. For example, she may cry every day from four to seven in the evening—right around your dinnertime. And, no matter how you try to soothe her—whether you pick her up, walk with her, or hold her—she may just keep crying.

If your baby does this, you probably find it very irritating. And that may make you feel guilty.

Your baby may not be a very "easy" baby. Perhaps she has trouble sleeping. The slightest noise may awaken her. And you may feel exhausted from being up with her so often at night. Or maybe she has a tendency to throw up her food, even after you've switched to a formula that should be easier on her stomach.

When you take her to the doctor for checkups and shots, your baby may scream the entire time. That may make you feel even more irritated.

If you have a baby who is very difficult to soothe and care for, you may even wonder whether having a baby was a mistake. If you have older children who were much easier to care for as babies, you may wonder what you're doing wrong this time. You may wonder whether you're even the right kind of person to be a parent. And just having those thoughts probably makes you feel worse.

## What Your Child May Be Thinking or Feeling

I hurt. Everything in the world seems to make me uncomfortable. Sometimes my tummy hurts so much from the formula that I hate eating. But I hate not eating, too, because then I'm hungry. Either way, I feel bad, and that makes me feel frantic.

When Mommy tries to rock me to sleep, the rocking just wakes me up. I'm tired and I do want to go to sleep, but when she rocks me, I can't fall asleep. I feel bad after she rocks me, but I don't know how to get her to stop. The more I cry, the more she rocks me.

I feel like something isn't working right. I need Mommy's help.

But even though I cry and cry, what she does doesn't really help me. And I don't know how to help myself, so I'm scared.

Sometimes I feel as though I'm going to explode inside. Everything feels bad. The sheet in my crib hurts my skin. If some-one pats me, it annoys me and that makes me jumpy. And when Mommy took me to the doctor's office, they hurt me with some-thing that felt like they were trying to tear me apart. The very worst part is that I have no power to make myself feel better.

## What It Means

Your child may need a lot of help either because she is very sensi-tive or because she is ill, hurt, or under stress for some reason. However, a problem arises when you are not able to soothe and help your child. The bond that builds trust between you and your baby may develop less strongly than you would like. And, as a result, your child begins to doubt that her needs will be met.

But neither you nor your child is at fault. Erase all ideas about placing blame: this relationship has no bad guys. A child may need a lot of help for several reasons:

- Some children are more sensitive than others—feeling, hearing, sensing, tasting, smelling, and seeing more keenly than average. All new experiences cause stress to the child. So the child's physical and emotional systems can feel attacked almost constantly. Your baby reacts to let the world know in no uncertain terms that she is feel-ing too much.

- Other times, children react to both food and airborne allergens that cause pain, congestion, and irritations of all kinds. Because of a young child's limited communication skills, you may have trouble figuring out what is causing your child's crying or screaming. As time elapses, both your nerves and your child's nerves suffer.

- Colic, a common condition many children experience during their first six months, creates high levels of stress for both you and your child. And illnesses of all kinds also inhibit your child from attaining the peace and comfort

upon which trust is built. Even after a condition is diag-
nosed, your baby may be forced to endure intrusive and
pain-producing procedures that leave their mark emotionally.

• Even the shots your child receives to immunize her against
some illnesses cause pain. Some children tolerate these
well, while others suffer more acutely, no doubt due to
their physical sensitivity.

Remember, no one means to hurt your child, and the doctor's
intent is good and constructive, but your child is hurt, nonetheless.
And during the first eighteen months, such hurt interferes with
your child's formation of trust in you and in the world around her.

However, children are resilient and can overcome much pain
under certain conditions. Incidents of hurt must be frequent to damage your child's trust. The pain your child experiences is not the only
obstacle to trust building. In fact, the main obstacle is your reaction
to your child's discomfort: how you modify the way in which you
handle your baby, and how you feel about her when she's upset.

Nothing is more debilitating for you as a parent than wanting
and trying to help your child to no avail. The strong, natural love
between you and your child creates an equally strong bond. But,
unfortunately, the same love makes you feel worse when you can't
or don't seem able to help your child. Don't be surprised if your
frustration and helplessness border on panic.

In turn, the feelings of helplessness can all too easily be turned
against yourself, creating self-doubt and guilt. You may think, "If only
I'd done such and such, my baby would be okay." Your mind may race
in circles, thinking, "I don't know how to help her." Circular talk
like this can leave you feeling confused, panicked, and overwhelmed.

You may even mentally strike out at your child—the cause of
your confusion and pain—or call her "bad." Rationally you know
better. You know that your child cannot help herself and that she is
only expressing her pain. Realize that your profound sense of helplessness and the anger you feel are the results of the connection
between the two of you: you feel what your child feels.

Although you may not be able to change your baby's discomfort
immediately, your reaction to her discomfort is within your control.

Know that the way in which you respond is crucial to your child's trust building. You are important to your child; she must learn that other people will meet her needs. Sometimes you won't be able to supply what your child needs, but you can give her your emotional support, physical presence, and reassuring words.

## What to Do

**Take care of yourself.**
You must take care of yourself. Otherwise, you will be out of control and unable to help your baby. This may mean bringing in someone to help you, consulting an authority, or talking to yourself reassuringly, reminding yourself that you are not to blame for the situation. Tell yourself, "I didn't do anything wrong."

If you ask a relative or friend to relieve you of your parental duties for a while, you may discover that all you need is company. If you do have to leave to clear your head or get some much-needed sleep, tell your baby, "I'm going to leave for a while now so I can come back to help you better. I'll be back at four thirty." Sure, your baby can't tell time, but naming a time will give her a sense of completeness.

**Stay with your child.**
Tell your child that you will stay with her. Say, "I'll stay here with you until you feel better. I'm sorry you're having trouble."

Next, tell yourself that you can help your child even if you can't cure her pain. Say, "I can help my child even though I can't take away her source of pain. I will simply stay with her."

**Pull out of your child's pain.**
Pull out of your child's pain by saying to yourself, "This is my child's pain. I will stay with her but I won't live her pain." Then tell your child, "Honey, although I can't take away your pain, I will stay right here with you."

**Give your child permission to express what she feels.**
Give your child permission to cry or scream. Say, "You can yell as loud as you need to yell to relieve the stress. I don't mind. And it doesn't matter what others think. All that matters is that you know I am here with you, and I understand you need to yell." Even

though your child doesn't understand all these words, she'll understand what you're trying to convey.

**Give your child hope.**
Say, honestly, "I know you feel awful right now, but you will be okay." Tell your child what is happening. Even though she may not understand the words you use, say, "The doctor is working right now to make you feel better. It won't be long." Or, if you are walking a colicky child, you might say, "We're walking now, and soon you will feel better. I'll stay with you until you do."

**Check your own ability to keep in control.**
Know how impulsive you are and honestly assess how much stress you can handle without losing control of your emotions or your behavior. Almost all parents have moments when they feel so frustrated that they think about hitting their child. But most parents don't actually hit or hurt their children.

If your impulsivity or temper gets out of control, beware of trying situations. If you feel justified in forcing a child to conform to your ideas of control, ask yourself why you need to wield power over someone so much more fragile and helpless than you. Is that how you were treated? Ask for help in these situations.

## What Not to Do

**Do not let yourself get out of control.**
The frustration and stress of having a child who needs a lot of help can get on anyone's nerves. If you want to physically force your child to behave, or if you want to mentally blame or abandon your child at this time, ask yourself whether your emotions are getting out of control. Seek help. Call a friend, a professional, or a crisis line.

**Do not let an authority figure separate you from your child.**
During your child's times of stress, you must be present if at all possible. Otherwise, your child suffers a double threat to her sense of trust. Not only is she threatened by her pain or discomfort, but she also loses connection with her greatest source of safety—you.

Often, professionals believe they can do a better job if parents "aren't in the way." Sometimes they feel children are less cooperative when parents are present. Both are true. However, though the professional may do a more precise, neat, or efficient job technically, your child's emotions will be more bruised, and long-lasting damage can result.

Remember, your child expresses her fear and resistance because she trusts you and feels safe to express her feelings in your presence. When you're not present, your child's fear of the unfamiliar people may stop her from expressing how she feels. Although your child's fear may cause her to cooperate in a stressful situation, your absence during such a situation may result in long-lasting emotional damage to your child's trust.

**Do not get down on yourself.**
When you can't comfort your child, don't get down on yourself. Know that your failure has nothing to do with your ability to be a good parent.

# Showing Fear

## Your Child's Behavior

You may notice that your child stiffens when he is startled. His legs and arms become rigid, his eyes open wide with a surprised look, and then he cries. This cry is different from the one you hear when he's hungry or uncomfortable.

You may notice this same startle reaction when an adult "roughhouses" with him—as when he is thrown up in the air and then caught. At first, if the adult is spinning around with him, your child may laugh and hold his arms up for more. And he seems to love the feeling of being swished through the air.

But if the adult tosses him in the air and then lets go, your baby may get that startled look that lets you know he is frightened. And he may cry and need comforting. When the play calms down, he may settle down and want to continue playing—as long as the adult doesn't let go and scare him.

You may notice the same kind of response at bath time. As soon as your child hears the water running, he may stiffen and pull away from you. But as you slowly introduce him to the water, he may relax and calm down.

At first, you thought maybe something was wrong with your baby because he seemed to get frightened from time to time. But now you realize that he's just sensitive to things that catch him off guard and surprise him: things that move fast, things that make loud noises, or situations in which he doesn't feel physically safe.

You have figured out how to help your child get used to these new and strange situations. You feel very protective of your baby, and you want him to know there's no need for him to be frightened.

## What Your Child May Be Thinking or Feeling

Being swished through the air by an adult is really fun and just a little bit scary. But if the adult lets go of me, then it becomes really scary. All of a sudden, I can't feel the adult's hands holding me, and the safe feeling I had is gone. My tummy feels awful, and I think I'm going to fall. I don't know exactly what would happen if I did fall, but it is a very scary feeling.

I used to feel afraid of water. I don't know why, but it scared me. It kept moving and changing, and it made me feel out of control. But slowly, I learned to feel less frightened. So now I'm not afraid when Mommy cleans me with soap and water. Mommy lets the water into the tub very slowly, and then it's not so scary. And I can see that when Mommy is in the tub, the water doesn't hurt her.

I feel safe with Mommy. She helps me learn about new things so I can feel secure. I trust Mommy.

## What It Means

Most children are frightened by one or more situations. Some children fear the dark, while others become overwhelmed and fearful around too much activity. Fear of water or heights is also common. For children to have fears is normal, and it doesn't mean you've done anything wrong. It also doesn't mean there is anything terribly wrong with your child.

During this stage of building trust, protecting your child from fearful situations is critical, whatever those situations may be. Pressing a child to overcome fear during this trust-building stage will boomerang, causing him to have more fear later. On top of that, the child won't develop a full measure of trust.

The most important aspect of working with your child's fears is to take situations slow and easy. Most children can overcome their fears by learning about fearful situations a little at a time. Remember, there's no hurry.

You must also protect your child from situations and people that are frightening or cause fear. A well-meaning relative may not understand your child's limitations and may inadvertently frighten him. Your job is to educate the person. If the relative doesn't listen, then your job is to take over and rescue your child.

Your failure to stop the fearful experience from being repeated does more damage to your child than the fearful experience itself. Your child must learn to trust you to protect him. Since protection is what your child needs, you help build his level of trust by stopping fearful situations.

## What to Do

**Calmly warn your child of potentially fearful situations.**
You know your child fairly well. That can be both a help and a hindrance. If you know your child is afraid of loud noises, for example, you may want to warn him when a train is coming. But the way you warn him is important. Say, "A loud train is coming. If you would like to cover your ears, you might want to do it now." This leaves the decision up to the child, and offers an appropriate choice for a child of one year or older.

Phrasing your warning in such a neutral way is much different than saying, "Oh, dear, a train is coming. Hurry, you'd better cover your ears, because I know how frightened you are." In this example, you tell your child you expect him to be frightened. Sure, he may be, but you want to give him the option not to be.

With very young infants, you'll have to offer the required protection. For example, if your child is startled by loud noises, cover his ears when you anticipate a noise, and do so until your child reaches an age when he can do it himself.

**Rescue your child from frightening situations.**
If an adult is doing something that scares your child, such as tossing him in the air, tell the adult to be more gentle or to stop. If the adult doesn't comply with your request or tries to tell you that children aren't hurt when handled in such a manner, say, "If you aren't willing to do what I ask, I'll take my baby now. Put him down." No arguing is acceptable.

**Soothe your frightened child.**
If your child is frightened, speak soothingly, telling him that he's safe with you and that you will not let anything happen to him. Sometimes, gently patting your child will help soothe his fears. Holding your child firmly, but not too hard, will help him feel safe.

## What Not to Do

**Do not try to teach your young child to be brave.**
Sometimes parents think they have to teach young children to be brave. During the trust-building stage, this approach is especially

harmful. It destroys trust you have built thus far and retards the further development of trust—and, ironically, the development of bravery later.

Such teaching is unnecessary, anyway, because children who feel secure and trusting automatically exhibit bravery in appropriate situations for the rest of their lives.

**Do not fuss too much over a frightened child.**
When your child is frightened, you want to soothe him. But don't make more of the situation than is necessary. As your child begins to settle down, you can begin to say less and hold him less tightly.

As your child returns to his normal state, don't continue to talk about the incident. Don't overdo it by saying, "Oh, my poor frightened little boy. Uncle did an awful thing throwing my baby in the air" . . . and on and on and on. Such talk is not reassuring. Rather, it reinforces the fearfulness.  Be matter-of-fact in your reassurance, and take your lead from your child.

**Do not let anyone make fun of your frightened child.**
Older children or thoughtless, insensitive adults  sometimes make fun of a frightened child. That is very harmful. They're trying to feel powerful themselves by putting the vulnerable child down. This is victimization and must be stopped immediately.

**Do not scold a frightened child.**
Others sometime think that scolding a child for being frightened will help him overcome the fear. Wrong. In the long run, such scolding creates a more-frightened child, who grows into an adult who also feels guilty for being frightened.

**Do not tell your child to be unafraid.**
Some people mistakenly think that telling a child not to be afraid will help the child not be afraid. This is a misperception. Fear is overcome with education, experience, and reasonable protection by trusted people, until the child becomes accustomed to the fearful event and feels capable of dealing with it.

You can say, "I understand you feel frightened. I don't see anything that will hurt you, but I understand that you feel scared. Would you like me to help you?"

# Appearing Lethargic

## Your Child's Behavior

Your fourteen-month-old baby may appear listless and just not look very healthy. She may not seem to have much energy. She may fuss a lot—not really crying, but just whimpering. When she's not whimpering, she may lie quietly in her crib, not really looking around. And when you try to feed her, she may only eat a little bit at a time. She'll take her bottle, but she may not suck it down with the gusto she used to exhibit.

When you take her to the pediatrician, the doctor may say your baby's weight is low for her age. And that may make you worry about her.

But the truth is that you may also feel grateful that your baby's quiet and that she's satisfied with staying in her crib. You would like to play with her more, but you're exhausted most of the time. If you have had a lot of change in your life recently (such as a new job or a move), you may feel you are in a constant state of stress yourself.

If your family has moved to a new home, or if the baby has been changed to a new day-care situation, those sudden changes in your baby's life may make her appear lethargic.

## What Your Child May Be Thinking or Feeling

A long, long time ago, I felt good. Mommy held me a lot and spoke softly to me. She smelled good. She would take me to places that were warm and sunny, and she'd laugh. She would tickle me and show me bright colors and kiss me all the time.

Then, everything changed. All of a sudden, I was in a new room and Mommy was not with me. She would put me in the car, but then she would be gone and I would be somewhere else. There were other babies and new big people. I didn't know them. They were different than Mommy. Luckily, Mommy would come back and get me after a long time.

After a while, I started to get to know the new place Mommy would take me. But just when I started to know the people there, they disappeared, too. Mommy would still leave me, but it was at another new place with a whole new set of big people.

Now I'm scared and confused. I don't feel good. Eating doesn't make me happy anymore. I feel like I'm going to choke. My stomach is tight. And I don't want to breathe too much because I'm trying to keep things from changing, but I can't stop what is happening.

I cried at first, but the person who came to help me wasn't Mommy. I don't want that person. So I stopped crying.

I'm afraid. When Mommy comes near me, I try to be very still and don't cry or breathe too much. I think if I just hold very still and don't breathe much, I'll keep Mommy from going away again.

## What It Means

The natural exuberance for life that flows through babies can be stifled by losses, including the loss of health and comfort, the loss of a loved one, and the loss of a familiar setting. Babies respond to loss the same way adults do—by grieving. And when a baby grieves, she doesn't develop trust that her needs will be met, because, in fact, those needs for comfort and security are not being met.

Signs that a child is not thriving, and, thus, not building trust, include fussiness and lethargy. In contrast to the bright-eyed, inquisitive baby who really lets you know what she wants, the child in grief whimpers weakly; she's lost her zest for living.

Obviously, any child may have some of these characteristics sometimes, such as during an illness or when teething. But if loss of energy and vitality lasts more than a couple of weeks, you should examine your child for physical or other causes for failure to thrive.

The building of trust requires a consistent environment with consistent caregivers who smell the same, feel the same, react in the same way, and do the same things. This may not be possible if a family is confronted with a crisis. Anyone available may have to fill in just to keep the basics going. But babies suffer, perhaps more than older children, who can be given some kind of explanation. Babies have no way to understand what's happening to them. All they know is they are not getting what they need to feel secure, which includes sustenance and tender loving care.

When a baby loses a special caregiver, the baby's whole ability to learn trust is compromised. Do everything you can to reinstate as much of the original caregiving as possible, or to substitute a consistent caregiver so that the baby can begin to build a new bond.

As your child becomes older (nine to eighteen months old), stimulation from the environment becomes increasingly important. Your child needs varying and stimulating sounds. Although a wide variety of sounds and music will fit the bill, make sure that your baby hears melodic sounds. If your baby is exposed to sounds that are too loud, too harsh, or too chaotic, her sensitivity to sound will be worn down, and she will begin to tune out what she hears.

Bold, strategically placed colors are important. A mobile, colored sheets, curtains, and stuffed toys all help your child distinguish color and shape. Babies are drawn to look at big color forms rather than little pictures that may appeal to adults. Babies can't distinguish detail, yet, and have no way to know what little squiggly lines mean.

Motion draws a baby's attention, and it begins to teach her about movement—her own and that of other things. Since your healthy child will want to begin to move herself as the first year proceeds, you will want to provide her with interesting things to which she will be attracted and want to move toward.

Finally, touch means a lot to babies. It's their strongest sense for some time. Your baby is aware of the feel of her sheet, her stuffed toys, your clothing, your skin, and your stroke on her skin. All of this stimulates your baby, increases her interest in her environment, and encourages her to develop.

Development is a strong part of trust building. Your child feels good when she can seek and explore what attracts her. When she feels good, she develops trust. It's that easy.

So provide your child with an environment that will continuously stimulate her growth; your efforts will help your child outgrow her dependency and set her on the path to becoming her own person. You don't have to push her, but you certainly can facilitate her progress.

As your child's trust builds, so does her ability to reach out into the world. If your child has suffered a loss, simply be aware of what she needs to get things back to normal. Once those needs are addressed, your child can get on with the business of growing.

## What to Do

**Check for losses if your child becomes lethargic.**
Notice if your child fails to thrive, appears to have lost vitality, or seems to whimper instead of robustly crying to let you know what she needs. Then consider what recent changes or losses have occurred in your child's life. Of course, be sure to have your child examined by a physician for physical causes.

**Keep your child's environment stimulating.**
Although you don't want to turn your child's environment into a frenzy of activity (that would be overstimulating), you do want to provide a balanced variety of stimulation. Sound, color, motion, and touch will all safely contribute to your child's growing curiosity. And as your child expands her perimeters, she extends her trust base.

**If you feel overwhelmed, get help.**
Raising a child takes a lot of work. don't feel ashamed to let someone know that you need help. You are actually courageous if you know when to ask for help. Even letting someone else take care of your child may be a heroic thing to do.

## What Not to Do

**Do not ignore the effects of loss on your baby.**
If you or your family is under a lot of stress or has suffered a loss, spend extra time getting support for yourself so you can better meet the sometimes taxing needs of your child. If you are unable to meet your child's needs, call for help. Try to ensure that the help your child receives is consistent and follows the healthy patterns you've established.

**Do not feel guilty if your baby fails to thrive.**
Sure, something is wrong if your child is not growing in a lively manner, but feeling guilty won't help the situation. Shift into a problem-solving mode. Start by asking for professional advise. Get help for yourself and your child. And always know you have options.

# Being "Too Good"

## Your Child's Behavior

Taking care of your baby may be very, very easy. You may even find yourself bragging that you can take your baby anywhere because he is absolutely no trouble at all. And other mothers may seem envious of you.

Your baby may rarely cry. He may let anyone hold him, without fussing. And even when he is very young, he may sit quietly in his car seat. He always seems to be very happy just staying in his playpen, looking at the lights and playing with his fingers. And he may seem to listen very attentively when you talk to him and explain what's going on around him.

Now that your child is beginning to toddle, he may rarely get into trouble. He changes his behavior immediately when you say, "Don't do that." You can distract him very easily.

In fact, your baby is such a "good" baby, that it may be easy for you to get distracted and not take care of him promptly. After all, he probably won't complain if you are a little late getting his dinner, so you don't really have to worry about feeding him exactly on time.

If your child is placid and accommodating, you may think it's because you have been doing everything right as a parent. You're reading child-development books, attending seminars about parenting, and doing everything you can think of to make sure you become the very best parent you can be.

## What Your Child May Be Thinking or Feeling

I like to see the interesting patterns on the wall. And I like to watch light—a lot. I wonder what it is and how it works. Sometimes Daddy talks to me while I'm looking at the light. I know he's trying to tell me something, but I don't know what it is. I'm happy just to have him nearby talking to me.

When I get hungry, I don't mind waiting a little while for my food. I don't need to cry or fuss. I know that Mommy or Daddy will bring the food sooner or later, and then I'll feel fine.

Sometimes, something bad does happen—like I have to go to the doctor to get a shot. But when that happens, I have Mommy or Daddy with me, so I know the bad thing will be gone soon, and I'll feel better. I didn't know why the nurse had to hurt me with that shot, though. People aren't supposed to hurt me. Everything is supposed to be okay.

## What It Means

Some babies are quite passive and easy to manage. This passivity is more due to the way they are neurobiochemically wired than to how a parent handles them. Of course, if a parent is hurtful or abusive to a child, or truly neglects a child on a regular basis, that child can become increasingly passive as he gives up hope of getting what he needs. But that is not what I'm talking about here.

The "very good" baby usually develops a large amount of trust that he'll get what he needs—and he develops it quickly. Because his level of need is slow to develop, he often gets what he needs without making a fuss. If your child behaves this way, you probably find parenting quite satisfying, for now, at least.

The problem with such a child is that he doesn't learn to communicate his needs clearly and assertively. He doesn't get a lot of practice. Right now, he's not expected to assert himself, but later in life he'll have to let others know what he needs, and he may have missed a lot of essential practice. The problem is, you can't ignore your child's needs just to force him to cry out for what he needs.

The good baby may also have a problem with gullibility later in life. Because your child has too much trust in people, he may be easily conned. And once taken advantage of, he may become pessimistic—the result of feeling that life tricked him.

Your child may also be more interested in mental activity than in feelings. Intrigued by his environment, how things work, and what things mean, he may not tune into feelings—his own or, later, those of others. To your child, the shadows on the wall, the sound of water running, how water runs through his fingers, or how a toilet flushes may be the most important things in his life—much more important than how he feels.

Nothing is really wrong with your child if this is how he is; he is what he is, that's all.

Your child probably takes his trust in you for granted. And being an attentive parent, you provide what your child needs so he can continue to develop that trust. However, other people may be much less attentive to your child, and since your child doesn't communicate what he needs loudly, he may be skipped over. That will damage your child's sense of trust later.

You may find that you will have to give your child permission to be less passive and more assertive. Many people don't understand that being quiet and undemanding is not necessarily healthy. Your child is better off if you don't want him to always be "good." It's in your child's best interest to become aware of his needs and to communicate those needs—even loudly, if necessary.

## What to Do

**Give your child permission to be expressive.**
Tell your young child, "Be sure to let me know when you are hungry (need to be picked up, want company, and so on). Go ahead and call me. It's okay to yell for me."

**Validate your child's communications.**
Any time your child cries, tugs on you to be picked up, or fusses even a little, say, "I'm glad you're letting me know what you need."

**Prepare your child for other people.**
When you get ready to leave your child in someone else's care, say, "Let Grandma know what you need." Or if your baby is going into infant care, visit the care facility several times so your child will get used to the new caregiver. While your child is in the new setting, say, "Be sure to let Suzy know when you are hungry. She'll be the one getting your milk until I come to pick you up after work." Be sure that the new caregiver talks with your child and encourages him to express himself in any way he can.

**Teach curious babies about their world.**
Some babies have a large mental curiosity, and they are very interested in the things around them. They want to investigate how

things work. You can help your child develop a bond to and a trust of people by becoming your child's teacher, as well as his primary source of nurturing. Make the learning experience a special time between the two of you.

## What Not to Do

**Do not get caught up in the "Good Child" syndrome.**
You will have to keep up your guard so you don't begin to talk about or listen to others say how good your baby is. All babies are good. Some have more needs than others, and some communicate their needs more loudly or clearly than others.

Don't reinforce the good child concept for two reasons. First, goodness is really not within your child's control. His behavior is simply a result of his capabilities. Second, sooner or later, your child will move into a stage when you may be less-than-pleased with his behavior. You don't want to judge that behavior as bad. It, too, is simply an expression of your child's needs, and your child requires your help to choose other ways to express himself.

**Do not forget your good baby.**
It is easy to overlook a quiet, passive baby. Be on guard so you don't forget about your baby. That doesn't mean you have to spend every waking hour attending to your baby, but you must keep a fairly regular schedule.

Also, try to have your baby nearby so you can talk to him even when you are doing other things. For example, when you peel vegetables at the kitchen sink, place your baby on the table next to you. Then have a running conversation with him: "Honey, I'm peeling these big orange carrots. See how long and narrow they are? I know you like carrots a lot. I mash yours up. I'll do that until you get some teeth to chew them up. When you eat carrots, you smile. That's how I know you like them."

During such a conversation, you've not only taught your child about the name and color of carrots, you've described them and introduced such concepts as "long" and "narrow." Then you spoke from a feelings-oriented, personal perspective. You let your child know that his smile communicates something to you. This conversation was a teaching experience, even though your child is too young to understand all of what you say.

Remember, information about how things work provides your baby with the building blocks to later take control of his life. For now, realizing how things work builds your child's trust in the world in general, and his trust in you, the person who gives him information that can help him get what he needs.

**Do not get caught up in the idea that your child's goodness is attributable to you.**
You are in for a big disappointment if you believe you are responsible for your child's good behavior. Sure, you contribute to it at a basic level. Every child needs food, tender loving care, feelings of safety, and bodily comfort. Your job is to provide for these needs.

But your child brings his unique personality and set of needs—beyond the basics—into the world with him. He also has his own style of communication and his own sensitivity to needs. You only guide the fulfillment of your child's needs, not dictate what they are or how loudly your child communicates them.

# Eighteen Months to Three Years:

## Identity

When your child turns eighteen months old, you will see a remarkable change in her. Suddenly, she will begin to say "no," vehemently. Your child will appear possessive and say "me" and "mine," regularly. You will also notice that she clings to you one moment and runs away from you the next.

In this section of the book you will learn how to help your child discover her identity—to see herself as a person separate from you—and how to help when she experiences separation anxiety. You will find out what to do when your child tries to separate from you, and how to help her so she will continue to develop her identity and independence. You will also learn how to react when your child is self-centered and possessive, how to keep her new identity intact, and how to assist her in acting in socially appropriate ways.

As your child learns about her body—what she can do with it and how she feels—she discovers more about herself. During this stage, your child learns how to do things by herself and how to make things happen; at the same time, you learn how to teach your child to respect things that are not hers.

Finally, you will help your child protect her identity as she opposes you, behaves aggressively, and appears stubborn. In turn, you can become your child's best supporter during this wonderfully energetic time in her life. By successfully negotiating the challenges of this stage, your child will know who she is and what she likes, and she will grow to become an independent person with a strong sense of identity.

# Experiencing Separation Anxiety

## Your Child's Behavior

You may notice that sometimes your toddler doesn't want to be away from you—not even an inch, not even for a minute. No matter how busy you are, your child may clamp onto your leg and just hang on. You may suggest that he go to play with some of his toys, and he may agree. But as soon as your child walks over to the toys and you are out of sight, he screams, runs over to you, and clamps himself back onto your leg.

## What Your Child May Be Thinking or Feeling

Mommy takes good care of me. She feeds me, plays with me, and makes me feel good with hugs and kisses. I'm a big boy now, and I don't always have to have Mommy carry me. I can walk away from her to explore things. But if I can't see her, I get scared. What if I can't find her? I have to let her know how bad I feel, so I have to yell.

Usually, it feels good when I leave her. But it doesn't feel good when she leaves me. To feel safe, I have to be in charge of leaving. But sometimes, if I leave her to go exploring, she doesn't stay where I think she should be. I can't see her anymore. Where is she? I didn't mean to let her out of my sight. That's when I get very, very scared. Sometimes I start to cry.

When I hear her voice, I feel much better. Then I follow her voice to find her. I run and run to get to her, and when I reach her, I hold onto her very tight. I'm not sure if I'll ever let go again.

## What It Means

As an infant, your child had no real idea of himself as an individual. He spent most of his infancy with you, and it was your hands, arms, and kisses that brought him what he needed. Your child knew how you smelled, how your heartbeat sounded, and how your finger tasted. In your presence he felt reassured and comforted. As far as your child knew, the two of you were the same person.

As your child continued to grow, however, his view of you and others began to change. He became fearful of strangers. At the same time, your child learned to trust that you'd supply him with what he needed to feel safe, secure, and good. With a foundation of trust in place, your child automatically felt an urge to take the next step in his growth—to separate from you and find his own identity. So at eighteen months, your child began to leave you, a little bit at a time.

Your child's tentative separations from you are an outward sign of his growing awareness of himself as a separate person. These separations also mean your child feels safe enough in the world in which he lives to risk spending some time away from you. The fact that he wants to explore is a healthy sign.

Your child now realizes that he can go where he wants to go, not just where you carry him. But that knowledge is also scary, because being away from you—for any length of time—can sometimes be very frightening for him. Your child still needs you very much, and so he has ambiguous feelings about his new ability to separate from you: he is excited, but he is frightened by the prospect of not having you right next to him.

A toddler responds to conflicting feelings by acting first on one and then on the other—back and forth. So your child runs away from you excitedly to explore the stuffed animal sitting on the chair in your friend's house, then he runs back to you in fear: he wants to be sure you're still there waiting for him.

Although your toddler wants to explore his world, he never purposely loses sight of you or of the trusted adult who cares for him. When he does manage to wander out of sight, it is by accident. And when that happens, your child screams from insecurity and fear.

From your child's point of view, he has to be the one moving away—not you. He needs to be the leader in his separation. It is okay for him to wander off from you a little distance, as long as you are in sight. But it is not okay if you wander off.

When you leave your child, he feels helpless. He's not independent enough yet to take care of himself. How can he even begin to get what he needs? Who will get him a drink of water or a cookie?

Who will hold him? What familiar person will make him feel okay?

As a two-year-old, your child often clings to you, to make sure you don't go anywhere. That reassures him you're right where he needs you. In a way, your child's new urge to leave you actually increases his need to be sure you don't leave him. Even though your child is going through a natural process, he is actually scaring himself with his new growth and change.

## What to Do

**Reinforce your child's feelings.**
Your job is to teach your child that he can be separated from you for a time and still be safe, secure, and happy. You can help your child deal with the very strong conflicting feelings he has about separation by both encouraging his exploration and letting him know that you will be there for him when he comes back.

When your child explores, tell him, "You are safe here in the house (or yard or day-care center)."

When your child clings to your leg, you can say, "I'm glad you're holding onto me when you want to."

**Give your child the gift of leaving you.**
By letting your child have the power to move away from you and come back at will, you teach him to be in charge of himself. This develops into independence and self-responsibility as your child grows older.

**Enforce some limits.**
Sooner or later, you'll probably get tired of your toddler clamping onto your leg. When that happens, offer your child a choice, saying, "I need to move around now. Would you like to sit in that chair where you can see me? Or would you rather sit right here and play with your blocks? Either way, we'll still be together." By giving your child a choice, you give him some power to get what he needs.

If your child still fusses and you have to get some things done, you can put him in his crib or playpen for a short time (no longer than fifteen minutes, please). But make sure he understands that this is not punishment. Don't scold him or shut the door to his room. Talk to him and maybe play some music. Be firm, but not harsh. Let your child know that you will return to get him. When you return, say, "See, I came back. I'm glad to see you. I needed that time to get a few things done. Now I can be with you again."

**Initiate short separations from your child.**
Although your child may not like you to leave him at this stage, sometimes you have to. Actually, short separations teach your child that you will come back. Tell your child that you love him and you'll return soon. Say, "The special person holding you will see that you get what you need. Be sure to ask her to put your special jelly on your bread. I'll see you later. Bye." Then leave. Don't look back or linger. Although leaving a crying two-year-old child is hard, your child will get over his unhappiness much faster if you get going. After a while, your child will learn that you do come back, time after time after time.

**Talk to your child if you're out of his sight.**
When you must be out of your child's sight for short periods of time, continue to talk to him. Tell him what you are doing; that may be enough to help your child understand you are still around. This is especially useful with two-year-olds who are in the clingy stage.

## What Not to Do

**Do not reject your child.**
Some parents, unable to deal with their own feelings about their child's separation, reject the child when he begins to move away from them. They may think, or say, "Okay, if you don't need me anymore, go on—and stay away."

If you think or feel this way, don't express it to your child. The urge to reject or push your child away when he tries to separate from you probably relates to your own childhood, when you were pushed to be independent before you were fully ready. It hurt you then and still feels bad now. But you won't really feel better by hurting your child, and you can feel proud that you are helping your child to separate from you in a healthy way.

**Do not cling to your child.**
If you cling to your child, you make it difficult for him to gain independence. You're not bad because you cling, but you do slow your child's development. Your clingingness may be caused by your own fear of separation. Or you may be overconcerned for your child's safety. Either way, the message to your child is the same: Don't leave my side. The world out there is not safe.

"Don't go there, you'll hurt yourself," some parents say constantly. "Watch out! Here, hold on to Mommy. I won't let anything happen to you." Even if you don't say these things aloud, these types of feelings can be transmitted to your child. Moderation is the key to a healthy separation process—realistic protection, not overprotection.

**Do not physically hold your child back.**
Never physically stop your child from walking away from you, unless he is in danger. And this goes for play, too. Some adults play with toddlers by holding them back as they try to walk or crawl away. That may seem like a game to you, but it can be extremely frustrating for your child. He will not see your actions as a game, but will, instead, interpret them as attempts to keep him from separating from you.

# Moving Away from You

## Your Child's Behavior

When your child was younger, she would either want to be held in your arms or to walk right by your side, especially if you were someplace unfamiliar to her. But now, your two-year-old may not even want to hold your hand. If you're walking down the aisle with her in a store where she's been previously, your child may pull her hand away from yours. She may even turn her whole body away from you and toddle away down the aisle by herself.

If you call her name, your child may move farther away instead of coming back. And if you go after her, she may try to toddle away even faster. Then she may glance back at you and giggle. The more serious you become about wanting her back with you, the more your child may laugh.

As long as she can see you, your child may think this is a very funny game. But if she turns a corner and walks out of your sight, you may hear her scream for you and then see her come running back. When your child reaches you, she may cling to you as if her life depended on it.

If you pick her up, your child may snuggle into your arms for a moment. But then, chances are, she'll want to get down and run off again. Once again, if you pursue her, she'll try to get away and hide, but the minute you are out of her sight, she'll probably want you back.

## What Your Child May Be Thinking or Feeling

I love to go shopping with Mommy. I especially like to go to our favorite store. I've been there a lot, and I know where everything is. I feel safe there. I don't need Mommy to hold my hand while we're in the store. I don't like her to hold my hand when I feel safe, so I pull my hand away from hers and keep it close to me. It's mine!

When Mommy isn't holding onto me, I like to explore the store. I start running away from Mommy. When I do, she makes a big fuss and comes after me. This really makes me feel excited! I feel so good, I run a little farther.

But all of a sudden, I can't see Mommy. It's too quiet. I can't hear her anymore. Where is she? Oh, no. I'm all alone. I can't see her. I don't know where she is. I didn't want to be all alone. I feel like I'm going to cry.

When I do cry, Mommy finds me. She picks me up and holds me. I love snuggling up against her. It makes me feel safe again. In fact, I feel very safe, and I realize I know this store. I've been here before. I want to get down and explore on my own. So I start wiggling and Mommy puts me down again. But I really don't need to hold her hand, so I pull it away and start down the aisle.

## What It Means

Your toddler must leave you to feel separate from you. At first that means she takes a few steps away from you, followed by a retreat back to you—three steps away, two steps back.

Although you might think that your child can't make up her mind, she is really practicing independence. Because her separateness from you is new, she has to test it in small doses. Too much space between her and you frightens her, at least at first.

Your child needs to keep you in sight. The minute you get out of sight, she becomes frightened. Your child's mental development still equates out of sight with out of existence. As a late two-year-old, your child remembers you when she doesn't see you, but as a young two, she needs to keep you in sight or within earshot.

Remember, your child is practicing independence. She will run away and come back over and over and over. As long as she feels safe, this learning will be fun for her. That's why she giggles. She's not trying to irritate you or make fun of you. She is simply having a wonderful, happy time.

When your child becomes frightened, she wants you to comfort her and help her regain a feeling of safety. She's learned to communicate her needs by crying, and she trusts that you will help her.

But because you comfort her so well, your child soon feels safe and is again ready to play the game "Run away from Mommy." So off she goes. . . .

Two-year-olds need to be in charge of their separation. Most of the time, they need to decide when to leave and come back, rather than have you direct the show. If you push your toddler away, she doesn't learn to separate with a secure feeling. And if you hold her and prevent her from leaving you when she's ready, she will feel trapped and will tend to rebel or quit trying to separate altogether.

Your job is to follow your child's lead and let her show you how much distance from you she can handle. Of course, you must be alert to your child's safety needs, which she is unable to judge at this age.

By age three, your child will be able to play separately from you for periods of time and will also be quite willing to walk with you. She will have learned about herself as an independent person who can afford to get close to you without losing a part of her identity.

## What to Do

### Support your child's separation from you.
Understand that your child is not rejecting you, but rather is finding out about herself. Be sure not to take her movement away from you personally. To the contrary, your child feels safe enough to move away from you because you did such a good job. Also, realize that your child trusts you enough to experiment with her independence. She believes you will still be there for her when she needs you, so she feels secure testing her new urge for independence.

Let your child know that you will always accept her back, and convey to her that she is doing something right, not wrong, by going and coming from you. Say, "You're a big girl now, so you don't always have to hold onto Mommy's hand." Or, "I'll be right here when you are ready to come back."

When your child runs away from you in a safe environment, tell her, "It's safe here to run off a little way. I'll keep watch for you." Because you give her independence at times, she will be more likely to respond when you notice an unsafe situation and insist that she stay with you.

### Support your child's return to you.
When your child needs comforting, reassure her that she can always come back to you for support. Say, "I'm glad you come back when you feel scared. I'll always help you."

After you hold your child and she again feels safe, she is likely to begin to wiggle. Say, "I can see you are ready to get down." One of the most effective ways to talk with your child is to simply reflect what you see her doing or wanting to do. "You seem to be feeling well enough to get down now." Then confirm that you're on her side, saying, "I'm glad."

**Provide opportunities for your child to explore.**
Plan specific times and safe places for your child to explore on her own. Tell her, "You're getting so responsible that you can be on your own here. I know you like to explore all by yourself. I'll be right over here if you need me."

All you need is a child-proofed environment where your child isn't likely to be in danger and where she isn't likely to bother others by her roaming. This environment must have easily recognized boundaries—your child won't understand such artificial boundaries as lines painted on the floor. The lobby of a small-town post office is perfect when other people aren't present. Closed doors block the exits and nothing is loose for a child to pick up. A child can explore and touch the mailboxes at ease.

**Stay in charge of the situation.**
Stay in charge of your child's exploration by giving her permission to separate from you. Say, "I'm glad you're ready to go by yourself. You are growing up."

To help your child stay safe, you can guide her by saying, "I'm glad you know how far to go and still stay safe. You know to keep me in sight, don't you?" This teaches your child the limits you judge to be safe, without forcing her to give up independence or power to actually be safe.

## What Not to Do

**Do not chase your child.**
Running after your child while you call her name only enhances the "game." Stop and say, "It's time to leave." Then take a few steps in the direction you want to go. Your child will follow you, though you may have to wait a short while for her to catch up. The more

fuss you make, the more you reinforce the game. Instead, be matter-of-fact, definite, and calm.

**Do not threaten to abandon your child.**
Never say, "Well, I'll just leave you here. That will teach you." Creating the fear of abandonment is a cruel way to try to get control of a situation. In addition, remember that your child's behavior is natural—not a challenge to your power and control.

**Do not scold your child for trying to learn independence.**
Realize that running away from you and hiding are natural urges inside your healthy child. Remember that your child's separation is important to her developing independence, self-responsibility, and self-care. Don't hinder this development—even when your child's behavior is exasperating (as when you're in a hurry). At those times, just say, "Today, you have to stay right with me because I'm in a hurry." Be sure not to say this very often, or the phrase will lose meaning.

**Do not overpamper your scared child.**
When your child runs to you for comfort, give it for a short while. Overcomforting leads to more dependency than your child needs at this age. She may learn that being independent is not okay and that, in fact, the world is too scary for her to venture into by herself.

# Being Self-Centered and Possessive

## Your Child's Behavior

All of a sudden, your child may start to say "mine" and "me" a lot. In fact, it may seem like he says that anytime his brother or sister comes near him or his toys. He may also say it when an adult approaches him. Even if the "toy" is a worn-out piece of cloth, your child seems to want everyone to know that it is his, and he says it over and over again.

Sometimes, your child even pulls things out of your hands—anything from the orange-juice pitcher to the diaper you've just picked up—and says, "Mine! Mine!"

You may also notice this new behavior when your child is with other children. If he's in day care or a mothers'-day-out program, your child may totally ignore other children his age most of the time. Or, he may walk right up to one child, take a toy right out of her hand, and say, "Mine."

If you try to explain to your child that the other child had the toy first, he may hold onto it with all his might and keep saying, "Mine," regardless of your explanation.

The same may also happen when you invite some of your child's friends over. At first, the children may get along and be happy—playing side-by-side, each with their own toys. But before too long, one of the children may toddle over and try to take another child's toy. One child may grab the toy and pull on it, while the other child holds on tighter and tighter, yelling, "Mine! Mine!" You may find that within seconds, both children are screaming and crying.

When you see this behavior from your child, you may find it embarrassing. You may wonder why your child is so self-centered and possessive. Can't he learn to play well with others and share the toys? How did he become so selfish all of a sudden?

## What Your Child May Be Thinking or Feeling

Everything I see belongs to me. At least that's how it feels to me. It's only been a little while since I started to realize that I exist. I'm just getting to know who I am. I'm me! I like to tell everyone that everything around me is mine: my toe, my mommy, all the toys I can see, and everything else, too. I like to play with my toys—all of them. They are part of what I know about myself. I feel safe with my toys, and I feel lost without them.

I don't care much about the other children because they aren't me. I want to explore about me. The other children just get in my way, and they take things away from me that I think should be part of me.

Sometimes other children come over and want to touch my toys. When they touch them, it makes me feel bad. It makes me feel like they touched me, and I don't want anyone to touch my body or my things when I don't want them to. I definitely don't want anyone to take any part of me away. That includes my toys.

Finding out about me is a big job—the biggest job I've ever done. It's so important that I have to defend every single thing that is mine. I have to defend it fiercely. And that's okay. I can do that. I *have* to do that.

## What It Means

Your child's job from eighteen months until age three is to become aware of his separateness from you and to discover his identity, which is innate but unknown to him. He must be totally self-absorbed to perform this enormous job. One way that your toddler learns that he is a separate and distinct person from you is to grasp his possessions to himself. That action helps him establish his identity.

Your child relates to everything and everyone around him in terms of himself. From this perspective, your child develops a sense of himself. His ownership of everything he sees helps him better confirm and establish his identity.

In fact, your child learns who he is, in part, through his physical possessions. When you hear him say, "Mine!" over and over again, you can rest assured that he is discovering his identity. His toys help your child to define himself. Whether those toys are new or old, or of any observable use, is irrelevant. They give your child the physical feeling that he exists. As your child touches objects in his environment, he makes them "his." That cherished toy that he holds with a death grip tells him something about who he is. For that reason, the toy is as important to your child as his name or his mommy and daddy.

Since your toddler experiences himself through possessions, he must keep them with him when he moves from place to place. Otherwise, he feels less secure and more alone.

When another child takes your child's toy, your child feels as though a part of himself has been taken, and that he will never get that part back. He feels as though he has been intruded upon—as though he has been touched in an unwelcome way. Consequently, your child will be content playing near other children only as long as those children don't try to take—or even touch—his possessions.

This normal possessiveness—a healthy part of your toddler's journey of self-discovery—often keeps children this age from getting along well together for any extended time period. That will bother you if you hold the erroneous belief that your child should learn to get along with others at this stage of development. You may feel a sense of embarrassment when your toddler won't share his toys, because you believe he should be able to share at this age.

If your toddler is in a day-care environment or preschool and spends quite a bit of time with other children, you probably want him to exhibit good behavior and not cause difficulty for the caregivers or teachers. But good behavior at this stage doesn't include sharing. Well-educated and trained caregivers understand that possessiveness is developmentally appropriate at this age.

Not getting along with other children doesn't seem to bother your child at this stage. Making friends is of no importance to him right now. His own journey of self-discovery is uppermost in his mind. If he seems self-centered, self-focused, and even selfish at this stage, he is—and it's wonderful.

When you realize the enormity of the job your child is undertaking, you will understand why he has no time for others right now. He will later, but not now. He cannot be bothered with other children, and when they intrude upon his job of figuring out who he is and what belongs to him, he must push them away.

Your child's self-centeredness is not a sign that he will grow up to be a selfish older child or adult. To the contrary, children whose natural development is respected, who are allowed to be possessive as toddlers, move through this phase and become respectful of others. As your child matures, even by age three, sharing will come automatically to him, with very little teaching other than watching you share. Your child will have a clear enough picture of himself to risk letting others into his environment. He will find that they can become friends. But children who are forced to share at this early age, when they have a tremendous inner drive to be possessive, are often very self-centered and possessive as adults.

A strong sense of self will help your child be self-protective as he grows up. And others will less likely be able to abuse or take advantage of him. In fact, because your child is developing a strong sense of self now, he'll also be more able to show concern for others as he grows older.

## What to Do

**Reinforce what belongs to your child.**
Affirm what actually belongs to your child. Say, "Yes, I am your mommy." You can add, "And I am your brother's mommy, too. I love both of you as much as the whole world." Make a dramatic sweep of your hands as you say this.

Go around the house and identify what belongs to your child. Not only does this help him learn what is his, but it teaches him the names of many objects. Remember, everything you do during this period should focus on helping your child identify what belongs to him.

Help your child by saying, "Yes, those are your blocks." Even when your child acts less courteous than you would like, affirm what is his. But set limits on the way in which your child lets you know what belongs to him. You can say, "Yes, that is your truck, but I need you to use a regular voice to say so. When you scream I don't understand you, and I don't like it."

If your child continues to scream, calmly lower your head or move away. As soon as your child quiets even a little, say, "If you scream, I won't be able to let you have the truck. You must use a quiet voice." Be firm, keep your own voice down, and follow through. This reaffirms the message that your child can get what he needs by using words instead of hitting, crying, or whining.

**Ask to use what belongs to your child**
Even you must ask to use your child's possessions. You'll serve as a model for him to follow. By respecting your child and his belongings, you show him how important his things are, which affirms him. If he says, "No," accept his answer without argument and say, "Okay."

**Set limits on what does not belong to your child.**
Be clear about what doesn't belong to your child. You can start by identifying body parts as belonging to you and not to your child. "This is Mommy's nose, not yours." Your child is not likely to be challenged by not owning your nose. Then you can move to the next step, "This is Mommy's bed, not yours. Your bed is over there." Walk to his bedroom and make a dramatic announcement, "That is your bed." You may want to clap your hands and act excited. Your child will love it.

When you're away from home, explain to your child what does and doesn't belong to him. "These blocks belong to the center." Then remind him of where his blocks are. "Your blocks are at home. As soon as we get home, let's find them."

You'll save yourself a lot of trouble by providing substitute toys for your child. "You can't have those blocks because they belong to the center, but here's your bear. Hold him tight." Always try to have something that belongs to your child.

If your child makes a fuss or throws the substitute down, you can say, "It's okay if you don't want the bear, but you still can't have the blocks."

If your child has a temper outburst, or whines, or does something else that you don't want him to do, say, "When you talk in a normal voice, I'll try to help you." Then, as soon as your child settles down even a little, say, "Let's go ask the teacher if you can hold one block for a little while. We'll ask in a normal voice."

By trying to understand your child's needs at this time, and remaining respectful of others' needs, you model behavior that your child will imitate later, when this stage winds down.

**Teach your child to respect others' possessions.**
Help your child learn to respect others' things. He may not be able to share his possessions, but he can learn not to take others' possessions. When your child grabs for another child's toy, say, "You have your blocks, and Jimmy has his. You can ask him if he wants to trade." If both children want to trade, help them make the exchange. Be prepared: the children may not want to let go of their blocks before receiving other blocks.

**Have a special area for your child's things.**
Have special areas of your house and playroom designated for your child's things. Even when children share a room, have a toy box for each, a special part of the closet for each, and a dresser drawer for each. Mark each item with each child's special mark. Use a sticker, a piece of tape with his name, or anything else that becomes the child's very own symbol to mark items.

In other rooms you may want to say, "This is where you can play, and this is where your brother can play. If you want to play together that is fine, but you have to ask first."

**Have only one child visit at a time, and have toys for friends.**
You may be able to head off crises by having a special set of blocks or toys that you bring out just for playmates. Your child is not to use them. This doesn't have to be elaborate—just have a few toys especially for friends. That way, each child has his or her own possessions.

Another idea is to have visitors bring some of their own toys. You can help the children exchange toys, saying, "Would you like to play with each other's trucks for a while? You can have your toys back whenever you want; just ask in a regular voice." As your child gets closer to age three, he'll begin to share automatically. Don't force the issue now.

**Help protect your child's things.**
When another child takes something that belongs to your two-year-old, help him recover it. If the other child is a young two, go to

him with a replacement toy and say, "Here, you can play with this, and I'll give back the other toy. That way you both can play." Then return the original toy to your child and say, "Here is your toy. Your friend didn't mean to hurt you. He just needed something to play with, and now he has it."

If two-year-olds get into a fight about what belongs to them, tuck one child under each arm and tell them that you will help each of them to have enough toys. If all the toys belong to one child, say to that child, "If you want your friend to stay, we'll have to find some things for him to play with. Would you like to choose which blocks he can play with?" That gives the owner of the blocks some power. If the child declines to share any, say, "Then your friend and I will play over here with something of mine." Soon the self-possessive child will probably want to join you and will be willing to give up a few blocks.

When a visiting child takes a lot of your attention and your child screams, "My mommy," pull your child to you, away from the other child, and say, "Yes, I am your mommy and I'm glad." Snuggle your child, softly purring your love to him. Then squeeze the other child, saying, "I'm glad you are visiting. You are very special." That way, both children get special attention, and no one feels left out.

**In a group, give each child his own toys.**
If several toddlers are playing in the same area, it's much better for each to have his own cardboard box than to expect them to share one big, fancy toy. The boxes can be labeled with their names, and even though the children cannot read, they can be told that their names are on the boxes. A favorite sticker can be added to each box to help identify the possessions. The children can sit in their boxes, ride on them, or put things in them.

**Allow your child to transport possessions.**
If your child has a death grip on a sock he picked up off the floor and won't consider getting into the car without it, let him keep it. If your child is playing with blocks and won't let go of a particular one at naptime, let him take it into his crib or bed. Letting your child take a six-inch wooden block to bed will do far less harm than prying it out of his hand while he screams, and leaving him feeling

that he's being whisked off to bed while a part of himself is being left behind on the floor.

**Support temporary possessiveness.**
The best thing you can do for your child at this stage is to respect his need to possess things in his environment. When you recognize and understand the driving force behind your child's behavior, you can relax and support what he is doing, and even welcome it. When your child refuses to share, tell him, "I can tell you really want to have your blocks. I'll find some other toys for this child to play with."

Supporting your child's inner needs at this time can help him become more self-assured and independent as an older child, adolescent, and adult. Your child will learn to trust his feelings and to listen to those feelings, as opposed to listening to negative peer pressure.

**Have realistic expectations of your child's behavior.**
Having realistic expectations of your child's behavior is especially helpful when other children are around. If you understand why your child feels the need to be so possessive at this stage, you will be less likely to be surprised or dismayed when he falls apart after a friend touches his toys. You can encourage your child to play near other children—toddlers tend to engage in parallel play, playing near but not really with each other—but you may as well be prepared for his reaction to another child touching his toys.

**Monitor necessary sharing.**
When toddlers have to share a toy, such as a backyard swing, an adult must help out. When your child cries and points to the swing that someone is using, you can say, "You want to swing? Thank you for letting me know." Then you can set a limit on the other child's time on the swing, saying, "You take five more minutes, then it will be my son's turn. He'll swing for five minutes, and then it will be your turn again."

Then you can tell your child to play with you for five minutes while he waits for his turn. If your child still fusses, say, "I will not let you swing at all if you fuss. You decide: Wait five minutes to swing, or don't swing at all today." Then follow through. Don't give in to fussing, or you'll get a lot more of it.

Talking, singing, and playing games with the child who's waiting will help distract him. Compliment him by saying, "You're doing a good job waiting." Then label him in a positive way, "You're a good waiter. Soon it will be your turn."

When five minutes are up, say, "Now it's your turn for five minutes. You waited well. I'll let you know when your five minutes are up." You must pay close attention to time when helping children share this way. Don't get distracted by talking to other adults, reading, or daydreaming.

Be sure the time limits you put on turns are short. If your twenty-month-old can only wait three minutes, start with three-minute limits and lengthen them as your child grows older. Some children can wait longer than others, and that's fine. Your job is to know your own child's limits and capabilities.

## What Not to Do

**Do not scold your child for saying "mine" or "me."**
When another adult calls your child selfish or scolds him for saying "me" or "mine," tell the adult calmly that in your family your child can say those words as long as he says them in a regular voice. Explain that you want your child to learn who he is, and that he is learning that now.

**Do not give your child things that are not his because he makes a fuss.**
Giving in to a fussing child, though tempting, is a very bad idea. The next time your child wants something, he is likely to fuss again. You are teaching him that the way to get things is to fuss.

**Do not force your child to share.**
Now is not a good time to try to teach your child to share. Your child isn't capable of learning that right now. If your child is afraid you'll disapprove of him or scold him, he can appear to share, but he cannot really learn sharing behavior he can use when you are not present.

Never scold your toddler for not sharing. A child whose possessiveness at this stage is treated as a discipline problem will learn that the driving forces he feels inside are not okay. He will learn that you expect him to fight against those feelings and do what other people tell him to do—even when those actions don't feel right to him.

**Do not worry about your child's possessiveness.**
Don't be afraid that something is wrong with your child because he is possessive and never wants to share his things. Actually, he's doing something very right. Remember, your child is defining his newly recognized self so he can become a mentally healthy adult who shares freely.

# Discovering the Body

## Your Child's Behavior

By the time your child is an older toddler, she may really enjoy bath time. She will be able to sit up in the water and may enjoy playing with plastic tub toys. She may like to splash and pour the water and watch how it moves.

You may notice your toddler looking down and examining her genital area. She may look up at you with a big smile and say, "My pee-pee" (or whatever name you use in your family). If you have a boy, he might have the same reaction examining his penis.

You may notice that your child has a strong interest in all of her body parts lately. She may love to point to her body parts as you call out their names. Maybe your child likes the game of comparing her body parts to yours: "This is my thumb," she says pointing. "And this is Mommy's thumb," you may answer. Your child may like to play the game of covering her body parts and having you find them. Or maybe she likes to play peek-a-boo or hide-and-seek.

You may enjoy playing these games with your child for a while, but she may want to play again and again. You'll probably want to stop before your child does.

## What Your Child May Be Thinking or Feeling

I have just begun to notice what a wonderful toy my body is. It's made up of lots of parts. Each part looks different from the others, and some of them move. See, I can wiggle my toes.

I remember when I first discovered my fingers. It took me a while to figure out that they were really attached to me, and it took me even longer to realize that I could move them when I wanted to. But then I began to discover all the wonderful things I could do with them. It's very exciting!

I've also noticed that Mommy has fingers and toes like me. It's fun to see hers. I like to play a game of hiding my body parts, or having Mommy hide hers, and finding them again.

I like to take a bath. In the tub, I can see lots of my body parts at once. I like to rub soap all over my body. After I play with my fingers and toes, I look at my knees. Last week, while I was looking at my knees, I found a new body part. It's down between my legs. I told Mommy about it. It sure is fun to explore.

## What It Means

Your toddler pays attention to her body as another step toward figuring out who she is. She is innately drawn to explore how she is made physically. Ever since she lay in her crib, she has been learning about her fingers and toes, how they go in her mouth to be sucked, how they move, and how they can grasp things and hold on tight.

By eighteen months, children's attention often focuses on learning the names of body parts and what they do. During this period, your child will become aware that her physical body belongs to her, identifies her, and is good (unless she's been taught through abuse that it is bad).

Your child will also learn to differentiate her body from yours, which further helps her see herself as a separate person from you. This leads your child to become self-protective later, as well as to respect other people's bodies.

## What to Do

**Play games that label body parts.**
With your child on your lap, point to her nose, saying, "Your nose." Then point to your nose and say, "Mommy's nose." From time to time, add another person, "And this is your brother's nose. We each have our very own nose."

**Show your child how she looks.**
Take your child to a mirror and point out body parts. Also, place her open hand on a piece of paper. Draw around it. Have her pick up her hand and show her the outline drawing you have made. Your child will be overjoyed. She can color it if she wants.

**Be matter-of-fact about all body parts.**
When your child begins the natural exploration of genitals, you must understand that from the toddler's standpoint, no difference

exists between them and her fingers and toes. Meaning is connected to these parts only in the eyes of grownups. Although the genitals of children can be stimulated, the physical feelings don't mean the same thing they mean to adults. Unfortunately, adults sometimes project their feelings and beliefs onto children's behavior, making a lot out of nothing.

Simply name all body parts with their proper names. "Yes, that's your elbow (or penis, or vagina, or tummy). And look, your elbow can bend."

**Teach your child about her whole body.**
As your child nears age three, have her lie on the floor on a piece of paper bigger than her body. Then draw around her with a marker or crayon. Go around each finger and toe. Have her get up before you cut away the paper outside the drawing. Your child can decorate her body pattern. Then you can hang it on the wall. It's fun to do a drawing yearly and show your child how much she has grown. Your child will get perspective on how her body changes over time.

Another good idea is to have your child look in a full-length mirror, so she can see herself as a whole person. This helps integrate her body parts in her mind, and provides her with a sense of wholeness.

**Speak well of your child's body parts.**
Although you don't have to overdo this, do speak approvingly of your child's body parts in a matter-of-fact way. "You sure have hands that can do a lot of things. Look how strong your hands are." Give your personal stamp of approval. "I like the way your hands are shaped. They're dynamite."

If another child is present, be sure to say something positive to that child also, "I like the way your hands are shaped, too." You can then point out the differences if you like, such as, "Your fingers are long and slender, and Sue's are short and wide." You are not evaluating either as better or worse. You are simply describing characteristics.

**Protect your child against thoughtless judgments.**
Sometimes family members, friends, and even strangers make comments about body parts that are judgmental and even hurtful. Usually that is not the intent but, innocent or not, such comments can contribute to feelings of discomfort for the rest of a person's life.

Often these are passed from generation to generation needlessly. "Too bad she has the Smith droopy eyes. It makes her look sad all the time." Or, "Look how big her feet are. I bet she'll have trouble finding shoes that fit when she grows up."

Often, grownups think children can't understand what they are talking about, but children do hear and remember. Many adults become needlessly self-conscious about the way their bodies are put together because of such experiences.

Say to someone who makes such remarks, "I'm sure you don't mean harm, but I'd rather you didn't talk about the way my child is built. She's just right as far as I'm concerned."

If the person becomes defensive, simply stay firm, saying, "It's okay if you don't understand. I know you didn't mean harm, but I insist."

## What Not to Do

**Do not scold your child for exploring her body.**
Most children explore themselves briefly during this stage, and if nothing more is made of it, they don't continue. The more attention or emotion you place on what your child does, the more you lock the behavior in place or cause problems later. If your child's exploration bothers you, simply distract her and go about business as usual.

**Do not judge body parts.**
Avoid using terms such as good and bad in relation to body parts. Simply label the parts by name and go on with your conversation.

Although saying only positive words such as "good" and "nice" when describing body parts may help your child feel good about her body, using such words does set up the duality of good-bad, and you may slip to the bad side during times of stress. So, try to avoid the judgment issue altogether.

**Do not make fun of your child's body.**
Even when family members tease one another, avoid teasing a two-year-old about her body. Remember, your child is going through a crucial developmental phase, and she's not tough enough at this stage to take the teasing without a lot of damage.

# Doing Things without Help

## Your Child's Behavior

Your child used to be content to stay near you. If you were in a store, your child would be happy to sit in his stroller and play with your car keys. But now that your child is a little bit older, you may find that he wants to explore and experiment with almost everything.

If you're in a store, your child may try to scrape gum off the floor, or he may try to open a grocery bag and put something in it.

You also may find that your child doesn't want you to help him as much as before. When your child was younger, you used to dress him every morning. But now, you may find that your child fusses when you try to dress him. He may want to try to do everything by himself, including things he can't quite accomplish yet. Sometimes that may frustrate him. But he'll keep trying. Your child probably has a lot of determination at this age.

## What Your Child May Be Thinking or Feeling

I love going to the grocery store with Mommy or Daddy. There are so many things to see. I see a reddish lump on the floor over there. I wonder what it is. I have to go see. I let go of Mommy's hand so I can run over there. Then I squat down to get a closer look. Gosh, it's hard to pick up. I want to pick it up and take it with me, but I can't get it off the floor. It feels very sticky. I'll keep trying to pick it up. I can do this by myself.

Mommy stopped me before I got the red stuff off the floor. I tried and tried, but I couldn't get it quickly enough. But I know how I can be helpful—I can put the groceries in the bag. I know how to put bread in the bag. I've seen people do that lots of times. Now I'm strong enough to do it, too.

This morning, I did something else by myself. I dressed myself! It was very hard, but I did it myself. Mommy used to get me dressed or

56

helped me do it, but now I don't want her help anymore. I can do it all by myself. I can put my clothes on my body. Mommy tried to help me by telling me how to do it, but I didn't want to listen to her. I want to do it my way. And I can!

## What It Means

One way your child figures out who he is is by finding out what he likes and what he can do. An innate urge to do things by himself appears during this eighteen-month period (which begins at eighteen months and lasts until age three). Your child wants to take care of himself and do things for himself. Such self-help skills are crucial to the development of your child's independence.

Your child also wants to learn how to use his body and its limbs. Running, jumping, and, later, skipping become skills that he and his body can accomplish. These accomplishments tell your child more about himself. Later in life, your child will feel comfortable with his body because he learned to use it now.

Your child will move a lot at this age. A nonstop whirlwind of activity, your child is discovering his physical capabilities. The intent is to discover himself and the world in which he lives, for it is his body and his world. When your child climbs the fence to see into the neighbor's yard, he learns more about what his body can do and more about his world. Your child is, after all, learning about his identity, not just from the way his body is made and how it works, but by his mastery of his environment.

The hardest part of allowing your child to do things without help is the time it takes. Trying to get your day going while your two-year-old tries to dress himself calls for large amounts of patience and extra time. Recognize the real issue and you may feel better.

## What to Do

**Point out your child's skills to him.**
Give your child a lot of opportunities to show off his skills. When he runs down the street, say, "You sure know how to run. Look how well you run." As your child gets a little older, he will ask you to watch. He may say, "Mommy, watch me jump." Whenever possible,

watch. Don't judge, but comment on how good it feels to be so skillful. "It sure is fun to be able to skip, isn't it? Your legs are very strong."

**Let your child do things by himself.**
Even though it takes longer and the results are often less than marvelous, let your child do things by himself whenever possible. Your child can learn to feed, dress, and bathe himself at an early age.

**Let your child make choices.**
Whenever possible, offer your child choices. Say, "Would you rather wear your red shorts or your blue ones?" Set it up so that either choice is acceptable to you. Put away things you don't want your child to wear or use now. Having too many choices creates stress for you and your child. Limit choices.

**Compliment your child on his self-help skills.**
"You did a great job dressing yourself this morning." It really doesn't matter how your child looks by adult standards of dress. What is important is that your child dressed himself. You are talking about the process of dressing, not how he looks.

**Childproof your child's environment for safe exploration.**
Because of the importance of independent exploration at this time, make sure your child has lots of safe places to explore, with lots of okay things to touch. In the kitchen, for example, have a sturdy step stool that your child can use to do things at the counter. If you don't offer a safe means to the counter, your child may risk falling, because he's going to climb on something to "help you out." You can say, "You may climb on this stool to help at the counter. You may not stand by the stove." Set safe limits.

**Set limits on unhealthy or unsafe exploration.**
Picking gum off the store floor is not bad, but it is unhealthy. Rather than scold your child, tell him, "Of course you're interested in that gum, but it's full of germs and could make you sick." You've explained what the reddish stuff on the floor is so your child can learn. Even if your child doesn't fully understand what you say, he'll feel your interest and know you are trying to help him. Then give him something else to do. "Come help me put this apple in the bag."

**Break down tasks into small jobs.**
A child can help if you break large tasks into small jobs. Although a two-year-old cannot button a sweater, he can help hold the button as you guide it through the button hole. Then he can pull it through from the other side as you push it from the back. You can say, "You are learning to button your own sweater. Soon you'll be able to do it all by yourself." Then watch the broad grin of pleasure and pride on your child's face.

## What Not to Do

**Do not continually say, "Let me do it for you."**
The two-year-old period can be awful if you try to control everything your child does. This is the time for your child to do things for himself. Your job is to encourage your child to learn skills and develop independence. Step in only occasionally, when you must speed a job along or when your child becomes very frustrated.

**Do not worry about things being done "right."**
When your child comes out wearing one white sock and one green sock, don't tell him he dressed wrong. Ask your child whether he would like to wear two white socks. If he says, "No," let it be. People will not judge you because your child has unmatched socks, and your child will learn to be in charge of himself.

**Do not scold or label your child as bad.**
When your child does something unhealthy, unsafe, or something that you don't like, don't scold him or call him bad. Stop your child, explain the situation, and give him other options for exploration. For example, if your child wants to constantly turn the knob on the television, say, "No, you may not do that, but you can sit here with Mommy, or we'll get out your knob set so you can play with those knobs." When you scold your child for doing something, you don't teach him what he can do. Every time you make a fuss, you reinforce the very thing you want your child to stop doing.

In highly dangerous situations, such as running in the street, sternly say, even yell, "No!" Grab your child, if necessary, and go inside, saying, "The street is dangerous, and you may not run there.

You'll have to stay inside (not as punishment, but as protection) until I can go out with you." Be matter of fact as you speak. If your child cries or has a temper tantrum, turn away until he begins to quiet down. Then repeat, "You may not go in the street. Yelling or crying won't help." Soften your voice and say, "You are precious to me, and I don't want you hurt." Then offer an alternative. "After I finish the laundry, I'll go for a walk with you. Meanwhile, come play in the kitchen." If your child still fusses, say, "If you keep fussing, we won't be able to go for a walk."

# Having Feelings

## Your Child's Behavior

Sometimes, your child may behave in ways that upset or embarrass you. For example, your child may kick and scream if you tell her "no" for any reason, even when the reason makes good sense to you. For example, your child may scream, cry, and kick if you tell her she can't go outside and play when it is very cold and raining, or have an ice-cream cone at six o'clock in the morning.

Sometimes, it seems impossible to please your child. You offer her something you think she may want, but instead of being happy, she may cry for reasons you can't understand.

Sometimes your child kicks and screams, but just a few minutes later, she may act like a baby again and cuddle up in your lap. And just a few minutes later, she may jump down from your lap and run around the house, making lots of noise. If you ask her to be quiet, your child may make even more noise.

## What Your Child May Be Thinking or Feeling

Something is happening all over the inside of me. If I need an ice-cream cone to feel good and Mommy says I can't have it, something just explodes inside me. The feeling just jumps out of me. Kicking and screaming helps. Whew, I feel better afterwards.

If something bad happens to my body, like if I stub my toe, it feels as though the pain just shoots all through me. When that happens, I feel helpless—just like when I was a baby. I remember how Mommy held me and made me feel better. If I hurt myself, I want to feel better now, the way I did then.

After Mommy holds me, I feel better. Then I feel like a big two-year-old again. I'm ready to get down and go. I want to run around and see what I can explore about myself and the world.

One time, Mommy said I was making too much noise and I should be quiet. She seemed upset, and that scared me. I like noise, and when I am sad, making lots of noise helps me feel better. So I make a whole lot of noise because I think that will make Mommy feel better, too.

## What It Means

As your two-year-old discovers her body parts and what they can do, she also discovers a new part of herself—a part that adults call feelings. From your child's perspective, feelings are something that she feels physically. This something propels your child to do things to express those feelings or to gain relief from them. Your child doesn't understand feelings as adults do.

You know that feelings create physical behavior. Sometimes you feel happy, sad, silly, and even mad, and you act accordingly. Your two-year-old isn't as sophisticated, yet. She only tries to figure out what causes the pressures and sensations that she experiences.

Developing a repertoire of feelings and learning how they effect behavior is part of being a two-year-old. Your child must learn to identify her feelings and learn how to acts as a result. When your child learns to understand and manage her feelings, you can then help your child control her behavior.

Because your child doesn't understand her feelings, they are displayed erratically at times, varying greatly in both intensity and style—happy to sad to heartbreaking. Or, they are displayed with pathos, as your child acts extremely pitifully. But you can count on your child's feelings to be expressed as big and dramatic, usually exaggerated out of proportion to the situation. Dramatics are the name of the game. For toddlers, the feelings are that big.

Your child cannot understand that you have feelings, too. A two-year-old is, first of all, self-centered. And you, after all, appear invincible. So if you need understanding at this stage, your child cannot give it. She can't comprehend that you could need anything. In fact, your child feels afraid when you show human weakness and tries to return things to normal in the only way she knows how, by doing what she likes to do.

Although not having the support and understanding of your child is tough, remember that nothing is wrong—neither with you wanting the support nor with your child's inability to give it.

## What to Do

### Teach your child the language of feelings.

At first, teach four basic emotions to your child: happy, sad, silly, and mad. When your child smiles, say, "You have a happy smile on your face." Then make a smile and look happy in return, saying, "Mommy feels happy, too. See? I smile, too."

Alternately, make a sad face and label it, then a silly one, and, finally, a mad one. If your child becomes frightened when you make a mad face, stop. Say, "That's okay. I'm not really mad at you. I'm pretending. Sometimes people become mad but they are feeling hurt. They try to protect themselves with their anger. It scares away their hurt."

Granted, a two-year-old will not understand the concept that you are trying to convey, but say it anyway. You will plant seeds for later understanding.

### Teach your child how to express feelings.

No one has the option to feel feelings. But everyone can learn options to express feelings. Your child is no different.

If your child screams (whines, pouts), wait to respond until she settles down a little. Never respond to a child's expression of feeling that you don't like. Wait, then say, "I don't know what you need when you scream (whine, pout). Use a regular voice to tell me what you want, and I'll try to help you."

During a quiet time when you and your child are sitting together, say, "My job is to help you to learn how to get what you need. When you scream (whine, pout), I can't help you. When you tell me in a regular voice what you want, I will do all I can to help you. We'll figure out something that will work."

Next tell your child, "If you scream, I'll turn my back and I won't be able to help you. As soon as you quiet down, I'll turn around and help you."

Your child may need only one time to learn this process, or she may need a few times. But follow through. When you turn away, do it in a matter-of-fact way—without anger, irritation, or great dramatics. You don't have to wait until your child completely settles down to turn back toward her. At first, turn back when your child improves a little. Later, you can require more improvement, until your child learns to communicate with a regular voice.

With very young twos, also use the turning away method when the child whines, cries, or frets to get something. Since verbal communication is not yet possible, teach your child appropriate nonverbal communication, such as gently tugging you on the arm or pointing a finger at the desired object. Once your child learns a word or two, teach her how to use that word to communicate her needs; for example, "da" may mean "there" or "that." Be sure to always respond positively when your child uses the word, but turn away if she whines.

**Reduce your stress level before it overwhelms you.**
The key to teaching your child how to manage feelings is to keep yourself calm—which is not always easy. If a day is filled with too much stress for your family to live peacefully, go to the park, get a babysitter for a couple of hours, or ask a friend to take over for a little while so you can take a leisurely bath. Do some self-nurturing. Remember to take the time you need to have fun as a family. Abandon your usual routines for a bit.

**Take your child's mood swings in stride.**
Know that your child has a wide range of emotions. Keep yourself emotionally centered when your child bounces off the walls. You don't have to fix everything for your child, nor do you have to make your child's life totally happy. Of course, don't create difficulties on purpose, but realize that your child grows from adversity just as much as from serenity. Comfort your child during times of family stress. Explain what's going on so your child knows she's not the cause of the problem, then stop trying to make everything perfect.

**Tell your child what you need and how you feel.**
When your child hurts you, tell her how it makes you feel, and what she can do to make the situation better. Use "I" statements. Say, "My head hurts. I don't like it when you make a lot of noise. I need you to be quiet. Thank you for helping me."

**Tell your child "thanks."**
Telling your child "thanks" even before she responds to your requests will help guide your child to do what you want.

You are teaching your child to be sensitive to others. Even though at least another three years will pass before your child can really empathize with people, you are laying the groundwork for your child to realize that others feel just like she does.

## What Not to Do

**Do not punish your child for having feelings.**
When your child displays feelings in ways you don't like, don't punish or even discipline her. Rather, use the event as a teachable moment. Rather than responding to your child's inappropriate behavior, show your child what you do want. Patient teaching takes time, but, in the long run, pays rich dividends.

**Do not use guilt to control your child.**
Although you may be tempted to use guilt to gain control of your child's expression of feelings, don't do it. The repercussions are similar to using physical force—an alienated child who doesn't know how to control herself and get what she needs in acceptable ways when she is older.

You use guilt when you use "you" statements to make your child responsible for your discomfort or displeasure. Don't say things such as, "You give me a headache," or "Look what you did."

**Do not mimic your child's poor behavior.**
When your child screams (whines, pouts), don't try to teach her a thing or two by mimicking. The lesson will be lost on her and will only serve to reinforce the behavior you don't want. Because your child's needs are not met, your behavior damages your child's trust in you; and your child doesn't learn what you want.

**Do not take your child's disinterest in your well-being personally.**
When your child doesn't sympathize with you or try to help you, don't take it personally. Your child's lack of sympathy doesn't mean that she will never be a socialized, empathetic person. She will, but later. Right now your child doesn't understand that you have needs and, frankly, she can't see past her own.

# Making Things Happen

## Your Child's Behavior

If your child has an older brother, sister, or friend, he will probably try to imitate that person. Whatever activity the older child enjoys, your child will probably want to try it. The results can sometimes be disastrous.

For example, if your child's older brother builds a model airplane, your child may try it, too—making a complete glue-filled mess in the process. Or if your child has seen his older sister put on makeup, he may go into the sister's drawers to try everything. If your child's older siblings get mad, your toddler probably won't understand what he did wrong.

Your child may also try to imitate the behavior of older children and adults in the kitchen. If you leave your child alone within reach of your spices, you may find every bottle opened and poured out on the cupboard. Or, if he can reach the milk, your child may try to pour it into every container he can reach. Although you would probably feel irritated at seeing such a scene, your toddler may not understand why you are upset.

You may also find that your child interrupts you constantly when you are on the phone. He may continue to interrupt, even when you have told him not to. And if you get angry at the repeated interruptions, your child may not understand why.

## What Your Child May Be Thinking or Feeling

I love my older brother and sister. They are the most wonderful people in the world besides Mommy and Daddy. I love to watch them all the time. I want to do everything they do. I want to be just like them.

My brother just finished building an airplane. I wanted to do the exact same thing, but I didn't know how. I got his plane down and took it apart so I could put the pieces back together myself—just like he did. I used lots of glue, like he did, and I worked really hard. But when he came into the room, he started screaming at me and was very mad. I don't know why he was so mad. I did just what he did.

The other day, everyone left the dinner table except me. I wanted to do what the grownups do. I've seen Mommy fill the salt shaker lots of times. So I thought Mommy and Daddy would be proud of me if I filled it up, too. When I opened it, a lot of salt came out. I was just getting ready to look for the new salt when Daddy came in. He got very angry at me. He said, "No, no, no." I didn't understand why he said that. No one gets mad at Mommy when she fills the salt shaker.

When Mommy gets on the phone to talk to people, I want to talk to people, too. So, if she is the only one in the room with me, I talk to her. I would rather talk on the phone, but talking to Mommy is nice too. Sometimes we play a game. I say something to Mommy while she is on the phone, and she makes a face at me. Sometimes I can even get her to wave her hand. It's a fun game to play, and I like being close to Mommy. But sometimes when she gets off the phone she is very upset—at me, I think. I don't know why. Maybe it's because she liked being on the phone, and she wanted to stay on longer.

## What It Means

As toddlers urgently strive to find their identity, they learn by imitating the people around them. Natural mimics at this age, children try lots of things. Their skill level is much lower than that of older children and adults, but they don't realize it. They just know they are doing "things," and their actions help them define themselves.

Doing real-life jobs, the same ones grownups do, seems much more fun than playing with toys. Your child likes things that have moving parts he can manipulate. Doing grownup things helps your child feel as though he has an effect on the world around him. Remember, your two-year-old is learning how to be a person by doing the same things you do.

Taking things apart is much easier than putting them together, even for adults. Your child experiences the same difficulty. When he takes things apart, his intent is not to be destructive, though adults often interpret it that way. The intent is to simply do something with this thing—to have an effect on the thing.

At this stage, a desire to do what grownups do is your child's biggest motivating force. During the next stage of development, at age three, curiosity will be your child's driving force as he strives to develop feelings of competence. But now, your child only wants to define himself. Taking things apart is one way your child figures himself out.

Adults often consider a two-year-old's behavior to be a nuisance. To be sure, your child's behavior can be quite disruptive, getting in the way of reaching your goals for the day. You may feel your child is "just trying to get attention," or that he is "being impolite," but these are adult interpretations that don't fit a child of this age.

Your child considers parents and loved ones as toys or objects with which to play and imitate. Remember, your child is self-centered now in an effort to develop his identity. Play is the way your child learns at this stage. He is just practicing.

So your child will interrupt you on the phone. When he gets a strong reaction from you, he'll interrupt even more. The stronger your reaction, the more he'll interrupt—unless you make him feel very afraid, which is not a good idea. Fear destroys trust and keeps your child from developing his identity.

## What to Do

### Teach your child boundaries.

The time has come to teach your child what is his and what is someone else's. Begin by defining the space in which your child can touch anything he wants. Often this will be his bedroom or part of a bedroom. If your child shares a bedroom, you may wish to put a piece of masking tape around the area of the room that is totally his.

Reward your child for recognizing what belongs to others, and help him protect what is in his area. You may use words, such as, "Let me give you a hug for respecting your sister's toys." Or you may wish to treat your child to an extra story at bedtime because he looked at the cake you made for your neighbor, but didn't touch it after you asked him not to.

### Set firm limits to protect other's property.

Teach your child to stay out of other's things by labeling them, such as "Brother's toys." Have older children put their important things out of reach until your child learns about boundaries. By the time your child is three, he will have learned much of this lesson.

When your child damages someone's things, stop him, tell him not to touch what is not his, and tell him to ask you if he wants to look at something.

Show your child an acceptable place or way to play. Often, you can give your child broken (but safe) items with which to play at this age, because he won't recognize the difference. He can play with his set of tools (leftover pieces of wood), while Daddy builds a carpenter's bench.

**Help your child "pay for his actions."**
Even though your child didn't mean harm, have him do something to "pay for" damage he's done. The payment has to be at a two-year-old level of understanding and ability. Also, the payment should preferably relate to the person who suffered the loss. For example, if your child breaks his older brother's model plane, the younger child may help wash his brother's clothes or clean his room. If your child gets an allowance, he may be required to give his brother a small amount to help buy a new model.

Tell your child about the payment in a matter-of-fact manner, rather than in an angry or scolding manner.

**Give your child adult jobs to do.**
Give your child safe jobs to do with you. Kitchen work is often a great place to start. When your child is two, you can safely provide him with a dull knife and a cooked potato and let him cut it in half like you do. Your child can wash or dry plastic dishes. He can help pick up and sort laundry. Many household tasks become learning opportunities for your two-year-old.

Although doing tasks with your child's "help" will take longer, you are actually accomplishing two jobs: the task at hand and the training of your child.

**Teach your child rather than punish or discipline him.**
When your child gets into something you don't want him to touch, you have a teachable moment. Explain the limits. Show your child how things work. Show him where or how he can imitate the task in which he is interested.

With very interesting things, such as television knobs, you may have to repeat the limits and options lesson for your child. Be a little more stern the next few times you explain things. If your child continues the inappropriate behavior and can't be distracted, he may be trying to communicate a different need. Your child may be bored or need attention. Try holding him or turning off the television and playing one-on-one with him for a while. If your child responds to the extra attention, tell him how to ask for what he wants directly.

Some children are very mechanically inclined and active at this age. They need a lot of opportunities to take things apart and do things. If you have this kind of child, nothing is wrong. But you may wish to spend more time with your child, for a while at least, until his skills match his interests and imagination.

## What Not to Do

**Do not overreact to your child's actions.**
Don't react strongly when your child gets into things, interrupts, and tries to control his environment. Remember, your child's behavior has a different meaning than you may think. Because your child tries to imitate you and reacts strongly to whatever you do, stay calm and he will also tend to stay calm. If you feel too upset to act calmly, go for a walk or to the park with your two-year-old, call a friend, or get someone to stay with your child for a while, so you can relax.

**Do not let your child play with valuable things.**
Place valuable or hard-to-replace items out of your child's reach. Since your child has no sense of the value of things, either monetarily or emotionally, you are responsible for safeguarding things until your child is older. Later, you can teach your child to restrict his exploration, but for now, your child must explore to fully develop his identity.

**Do not discourage your child from doing real things.**
don't restrict your child from imitating you, or tell him to "go play like a child." This only teaches your child that he shouldn't be independent and responsible like a grownup. Support your child's attempts by providing safe ways for him to work by your side.

# Opposing You

## Your Child's Behavior

You may notice that "no" is suddenly your child's favorite word. No matter what you ask her, her first answer is "No." Whatever you say or suggest, your child says the opposite. And chances are, you're getting a little tired of your child's behavior.

If you suggest that your child sit at a certain place at the table, she may answer with, "No. I sit there," as she points across the table. If you suggest a certain shirt for her to wear, she may say loudly, "No. I won't wear it."

If you want your child to sit still in a restaurant, she may bang her spoon on the table, scoot down from her seat, crawl under the table, or walk around the restaurant. Before you can catch her, your child may run right into someone carrying a plate of food. When you do catch up to your child and pick her up, she may yell in protest as loudly as she can, getting the attention of everyone in the restaurant.

If your child behaves this way, her behavior is probably embarrassing to you. And you probably can't quite figure out what it all means.

## What Your Child May Be Thinking or Feeling

The whole world seems to be against me. Even Mommy and Daddy, whom I trust, keep getting in my way. They are always trying to stop me, tell me what to do, and make me do things that I don't want to do.

I have a mind of my own. It belongs to me. I will stick by that—and tell the whole world if I have to. I'm becoming very strong.

So, when Mommy and Daddy tell me to do things that I don't want to do, I have to say, "No." If I don't, I feel helpless, as though I'm only a part of Mommy and Daddy. But I'm my own person. Saying no helps me feel that I'm my own person and that I'm strong. It makes space between me and them. I have to be separate to make sure that I can feel me.

Sometimes I have to argue with Mommy and Daddy to stay connected to them. I know I want to be a little bit separate from them, but not too separate.

In the restaurant, for example, I know where I want to sit, and I know what I want to eat. I want people to know that I'm me and that I'm here, so I make a lot of noise on the table with my spoon. It makes a very good, loud noise.

When I finish eating all I want, I have to do something else. I hate just sitting. It hurts me inside to sit still for too long. When I get that feeling, I know how to take care of it. I just slide down, scoot under the table, and find someone else to talk to, or something else to explore. Then I feel better.

I hate sitting around while grownups talk. I don't mind it if everyone knows I feel that way. I want them to know.

## What It Means

During the early part of this stage, which lasts from eighteen months to age three, your child will not only say no at the drop of a hat, but will seem unable to say yes. Your child will refer to herself as "me"—"Me do it." Your child will be nearly three years old before she can say "I," and interestingly, she'll also begin to say yes, sometimes.

During part of this eighteen-months period, your child's need to be in charge of herself and of everything she does will rise to a peak. That is when your child will be most resistant to help from you, most offensive in all social situations, and least pleasant anyplace that requires restriction on her freedom.

Fortunately, the peak of this period is short, often a month or two. But it is stressful and wearing on those around the child. Don't feel as though you have done a poor parenting job. In fact, the strength of your child's resistance is often in proportion to how safe she feels exerting herself around you.

Ironically, many people see just the opposite, thinking that something is very much wrong in the family of the resisting child. You must realize that your child is communicating strongly, though not acceptably, to you. Then realize that, by her resistance, your child is showing you a strong sense of loyalty to herself. This loyalty is important because from it comes independence and a strong sense of self as separate from others. This sense will protect your child later from suggestibility or easy influence.

Arguing with you allows your child to build her emotional muscle. Make sure that she wins sometimes. Forcing a two-year-old to wear something she doesn't want to wear proves that you are stronger than her, but it also damages your child's trust in you and retards the process of discovering and strengthening of identity. You and your child will pay for this damage later, when your child is a teen and an adult who can't make up her mind, is suggestible, and lacks independence and leadership skills.

If you spend most of your time teaching your child how to be her own boss, this difficult period will not last long; while the period during which your child develops identity will still last from eighteen months to three years, the oppositional behavior of this period will subside quicker. When you teach your child how to be her own boss, also teach her the limits within which she can be her own boss.

Some children are stronger willed than others. That doesn't mean anything is wrong with them, you, or your parenting. Please don't label your children in any way. A lot of the manner in which children express themselves is neurologically based and may even be genetic. Work with your child, and be sure you are not the one who has to have your own way.

## What to Do

**Have a few clear limits.**
Choose your battlefields wisely. Select only a few areas, mostly those that are dangerous or intrusive to other people, to insist that your child does things your way. Otherwise, let your child take the lead.

**Choose carefully where you take your child.**
Spare yourself and your child unnecessary frustration, and spare others the unnecessary disturbance of putting up with your child during her peak opposition period. This peak only lasts a couple of months, so during that time, have picnics in the park instead of eating in a restaurant. Your child will learn to be a socially acceptable person later—with her identity intact.

**Affirm your child's "no" statements.**

When you ask your child to do something, such as, "Put your clothes in the laundry basket," and she says, "No," say, "Okay," or "You don't want to do it now." If you don't make a big deal out of your child's "no," she will probably do what you've asked within a few minutes.

If, after a while, your child's clothes don't appear in the laundry basket, give her a choice, "Would you rather put your clothes in the laundry basket now, or before your story." A choice gives your child power. She wins either way.

**Teach your child to say what she wants.**

When your child says no, ask her what she does want or how she wants to do something. If your child says no to French fries in a restaurant, say, "What would you like to eat?" If your child says nothing, she probably doesn't know. Give her a choice: "Would you like spaghetti or rice?" If she still says no, she may not be hungry. You can say, "It's okay if you don't want anything now, but this is dinner and you may get hungry later. If you would like to order now, you can taste your food, and then we'll get a doggie bag and take the rest home for later." Do *not* go home and cook a separate meal for your child. She has to go along with the situation, but she can have her own timetable.

**Affirm your child's negative choices.**

When your child says yuk or no to green beans, say, "You definitely know what you like and what you don't like. I can tell you're someone who doesn't like green beans now." When you don't argue with her, your child will realize that others understand how she feels and what she likes, and she won't have to fight so hard to get her point across. By adding the word "now," you open the door for your child to change her mind later without losing face.

**Teach your child how to communicate her opposition appropriately.**

The manner in which your child communicates her opposition is important. Temper tantrums, screaming, and whining are not acceptable because they are socially irritating and won't get your child what she wants later in life. By using regular words in a moderate voice, you teach your child acceptable ways to communicate. She will respond in a like manner, free from having to make a big fuss.

**Protect your child from overcontrolling people.**
Many families have a member who believes children should be seen and not heard, and that they should not be allowed to have any say in their lives. When such a person speaks to you or your child, say, "Thank you for your concern, but in our family our child is allowed to speak up." If the person continues to criticize you or your child, say, "I do things differently from you, and I'd appreciate your not saying any more. Thank you."

## What Not to Do

**Do not get in a power struggle with your child.**
Arguing sets up a situation in which the child always loses. If you win, your child loses her power to assert herself. If your child wins, she loses a strong adult who can guide her. Either way, your child loses. So avoid the power struggle by giving your child choices. Even if she doesn't make a choice, you can still have limits. "Okay, you don't have to eat now, but you should know that I'm not cooking later."

**Do not punish your child for opposing you.**
When your child resists you, affirm her opinions and wishes, saying, "You know what you like. I'm glad you're telling me." Remember, your child is building independence and emotional strength. Do enforce your limits, however.

**Do not allow your child to be abusive to you or to others.**
Your child must not be allowed to be abusive or intrusive to others or to break up an otherwise peaceful gathering. Say, "You may not interrupt." You may want to use a time-out if your child persists.

Be sure that your child has someone to help her meet her needs and that the setting fits the age of your child. Expecting a child to sit quietly for an hour after dinner while grownups talk is not reasonable.

# Behaving Aggressively

## Your Child's Behavior

As your toddler begins to spend more time in the company of other children, whether they're friends from the neighborhood, preschool, or day care, you may find that sometimes the children get along well, and sometimes they don't.

Even though you've talked to your child about the rules of getting along with others, you may find that he occasionally pushes, hits, or even bites other children.

## What Your Child May Be Thinking or Feeling

I love doing special things with Mommy. One of the most special things we do is go to the park. Usually Mommy sits on a blanket and I play in the sandbox nearby. I like playing in there alone so all the toys and the sand can be mine.

Sometimes another child comes along and climbs in the sandbox. Then he tries to make everything in the sandbox his. I don't like that. If he tries to touch my toys or play with my sand, I get very mad.

Sometimes, if someone makes me very mad, I have to be my strongest against them, to show them that they should never try to touch my toys again. When that happens, I use my teeth. The other child may scream and cry, but he usually goes away, or an adult comes to get him.

## What It Means

As your child develops his sense of self, he quickly discovers that he must protect it. Since your child's sense of self involves his body, what he can do with it, his feelings, and the things that belong to him, any intrusion into any of these areas causes your child to feel threatened. After all, his very existence is challenged.

Yet, your child has few self-defense skills. The strongest and most developed, especially for young two-year-olds, involves teeth. Your child quickly learns that teeth are strong and get action quickly.

Your child can also defend himself by pushing, shoving, and hitting, though the effectiveness of these actions depends somewhat on your child's physical size and strength compared to the other child's.

A child of this age is not mean, mean-spirited, evil, or bad. These adult explanations for behavior are based on the assumption that a child has developed empathy for others. Empathy doesn't develop until the last stage of emotional development, around age five. From the perspective of your two-year-old, another child doesn't appear much different from a block or any other object. When that child does something to your two-year-old, he has to defend himself.

Although sometimes children act aggressively at this age because they are defending themselves and their things, sometimes they act aggressively for another reason. When your child's world is more stressful than usual, he will often react aggressively. For example, if your home is being remodeled, your child will be stressed by the changes in his home, and he will also feel his parents' stress. Even when parents don't verbalize their worries or stresses, children pick them up like radar.

Parents may be worried about the finances or mess connected with remodeling, though they may not say anything. The child will sense their anxiety. Because two-year-olds have so little experience with stress, they are easily overwhelmed by it. When they feel out of control, they strike out.

Children are like sponges at this age. They will absorb any feelings you have, even those you don't express openly, and act them out for you. So if you're mad at your spouse but are not saying anything, your child is likely to act more angrily and aggressively than usual to discharge the tension in the air.

## What to Do

### Stop the aggression.
Understand your child's aggressive behavior, but don't condone it or allow it to continue. Your first job is to stop the aggression—but not with more aggression. Children are at their peak of imitative learning. When you hit, spank, or beat a child, at this age or at any other time, you teach the child to be physically violent.

Immediately attend to the injured or hurt child. Then turn to the aggressor and say, "You may not bite (hit, kick). When you don't like something, let me know. I'll help you protect your things."

**Look for a reason for the aggression.**
Before you decide what to do in response to your child's aggression, you must know the reason for it; otherwise you may treat the wrong cause. Check whether your child has to be taught other self-defense skills or whether he is responding to too much stress in his environment.

Ask yourself and your child what is different at home or at preschool or in the neighborhood. Look for everyday changes, not necessarily bad or stressful occurrences, just any changes. Your child's stress could be the result of a beloved big brother going off to college or even a promotion for you.

Before speaking to your child about his behavior, be sure to assess how you feel. Remember, children at this age pick up and play out your feelings.

**Teach your child self-defense skills.**
Tell your child to use words when another child takes something that belongs to him. "Say, 'No,' when you don't like something."

Tell your child to come to you, his teacher, or another adult if someone is bothering him; tell him the adult will help him.

**Teach your child ways to recognize and reduce his stress.**
Tell your child, "When you get tired of people coming into your house and moving your things, let me know and we'll go for a walk or go swimming to get away from the mess." This teaches your child to do something about stress, and suggests alternatives that he can use.

**Have consequences for your child's aggressive behavior.**
Your child's aggressive behavior must be stopped in a nonaggressive way. A brief time-out often works well. Sending a two-year-old to his room for two minutes or having a time-out chair in which your child must sit can do the trick.

Time-outs should be very short at this age. Longer time-outs fail to serve the intended purpose of teaching your child. Not only will your child not understand what you are trying to accomplish, but he will experience your actions as hurtful and unfair. This breaks trust and builds angry feelings inside him. Those feelings will surface years later as rebellion, or they will be displaced onto other people.

If your child continues to act aggressively after a brief time-out, change his situation. If your child has a friend over, the friend may have to go home. Say to your child, "You seem to be having a hard time controlling yourself today. Your friend will have to go home."

Follow through despite tears or protests. Your child must learn that you will follow his aggression with action.

If your child's level of aggression increases or continues over a long period of time, it may be a symptom of abuse, trauma, or undue stress. Check your child's situations, and consider visiting a counselor.

## What Not to Do

**Do not use aggression to control your child.**
Don't respond to your child's aggression with aggression—physical or mental. This approach teaches the wrong lesson. Your don't have to use brute force to get your child to do what you want.

**Do not force your child to trade his identity for your approval.**
Your child wants your approval, but not at the expense of his identity. Don't put your child in that position. Show him how to get what he needs *and* get your approval. Be clear about how to please you, saying, "When you talk in a regular voice, I want to help you. When you hit, I don't want to help you, and I won't."

**Do not allow your child to bully others.**
A child who is out of control, bullying others, is a child who will be ostracized before long. Part of your job as a parent is to help your child fit into social situations. You can teach your child by saying, "When you hit your friend, it makes him feel bad. He won't want to be your friend any more."

Then be sure to tell your child what to do: "If you don't want your friend to play with your toy, give him one he *can* play with."

**Do not try to make your child feel guilty.**
Purposely trying to instill guilt as a way to control your child's behavior damages your child's good feelings about himself.

Although guilt may appear to work in the short run, the cost is your child's self-esteem. Take a little longer to teach your child how to get what he needs, and your child will keep his self-esteem and self-control.

# Being Stubborn

## Your Child's Behavior

Sometimes your child can be so stubborn and say "No" so often that it ruins your mood and spoils your plans.

For example, suppose it's the dead of winter and you want to take your child to the mall to get out of the house. That may seem like a great plan to you, with one exception: Your child insists that she wear her swimsuit. You may try to reason with your child and explain how cold it is outside, but there's a good chance that nothing you say will convince your child that wearing a swimsuit is a bad idea.

At first, you may try to patiently coax your child into being sensible, but that may not work. The more you urge your child, the more stubborn she may become.

Even if you threaten to take something away—either a toy or an activity that your child likes—she still may not give in. By the end of this verbal tug-of-war, your child may be in a crying heap on the floor—still clutching her swimsuit.

## What Your Child May Be Thinking or Feeling

I really like going places with Mommy and Daddy. When I do, I like to wear my favorite things. My clothes show everyone who I am, and I feel good inside when I wear them. I feel proud. My very favorite thing to wear is my swimsuit. It makes me really happy!

Sometimes my parents won't let me wear it. They get mad. I get mad, too. I'm me, and I know what I like. I know that wearing my swimsuit would be the very best thing for me to do. Mommy and Daddy don't know what's best for me. I do. I'll show them I'm right. When I put on my swimsuit, they'll see how happy I am.

If I do what they want instead of what I know is best, I'll lose control of a part of me. I can't do that. I have to insist on wearing my swimsuit. I feel safe in my swimsuit. The more Mommy and Daddy tell me I must wear something else to go to my favorite place, the more confused I feel. I don't know what to do. I feel helpless. Now I may lose everything.

## What It Means

Because your child is in the process of defining herself by what she wears and by the choices she makes, she must hold onto them stubbornly. When she does, it is a sign of strength; the strength of her convictions and commitment to being her own person.

Although some of your child's choices may seem senseless to you, they have great meaning to her. Your child simply doesn't think rationally, the way you do. Instead, your child responds emotionally to a symbol that represents her. So the fact that the temperature outside is freezing has nothing to do with your child's choice to wear a swimsuit.

Neither is your child's stubbornness against you. Although you may create the situation that your child has to buck, your child resists the *situation*, not *you*, to protect her way of doing things.

Strength of character and the ability to stand up for what she believes will be the offshoots of your child's current stubbornness. Welcome it. Your child will be less suggestible because she knows who she is and what she wants. Your child will let go of her stubbornness when she feels stronger inside and has more skills to communicate and negotiate.

## What to Do

**Help your child figure out how to get what she thinks she needs.** If your child wants to wear her swimsuit, acknowledge her desires by saying, "I can see you love your swimsuit and that you want to wear it." Then present your child with information that you think is important, such as, "It's cold outside."

Next, make any personal statements that you wish. "I like to wear my swimsuit in the warm weather." You've used the word "I" rather than saying, "People do it," or "You should do this." You've also introduced the connection between swimsuits and warm weather. Earlier, you told your child it was cold, so you've noted the difference.

Without trying to talk your child out of her desire, tell her you will help her figure out how to do what she wants and still be comfortable. Say, "If you want to wear your swimsuit, I'll try to help you figure out a way to do that and still stay warm. Maybe you could wear it over your long pants. Or maybe you could wear long pants over it." (Remember, how your child looks isn't important at this time. Think of it as wearing a costume, though don't say that to her.)

Finally take the big risk. Ask your child's opinion. That gives her the power she needs at this time. "Do either of these ideas sound okay to you?" Most times your child will take one, since she doesn't lose power by making a choice, and she gets to wear her swimsuit.

**Let your child experience the consequences of her desires.**
As long as your child is not in danger of hurting herself, let her experience the consequences of her desires—and don't laugh at her or put her down. If your child insists on only wearing her swimsuit, realize that she makes the decision from inside a warm house. Let your child go out in her swimsuit. You may say, "You must wear socks and shoes."

Then nonchalantly add, "I'll throw your long pants and a sweater in the back seat in case you decide you want them." In all probability, the pants and sweater will be pulled on within seconds. When they are, don't say, "I told you so." That robs your child of power and only proves to her that you are more powerful. Your child already knows that—now she's learning about her own power, not yours.

**Teach your child the difference between everyday and emergency situations.**
Sometimes you must pull rank and your child must do what you say, now. Tell your child that most of the time you'll help her do what she wants, but once in a while she'll have to do what you want, immediately. For example, go through fire drills—yes, even at two. Speak so you don't overly frighten your child, "We work hard to keep our house safe, but if it catches on fire, we have to leave immediately. I will tell you what to do, and you must do it right away—no choices."

Then role-play the situation, with your child instantly responding to what you say. Practice the fire drill. Your two-year-old will sense the difference from everyday events. Tell your child how important her quick response is.

Even in less-threatening situations, such as being late for work, introduce the word "important." Use this word only occasionally. If you're late for work on a daily basis, your words will lose effectiveness. You must revamp your schedule.

## What Not to Do

**Do not get in a power struggle with your child.**
When you try to prove to your child that you are stronger, you join her level of inexperience. Ask yourself whether you were ever allowed to win as a child. If your answer is no, be kind to yourself, but don't expect to get what you need at you child's expense.

Remember, everyone loses in a power struggle, no matter how it works out.

**Do not use force or fear to make your child obey you.**
When you use force or fear, you teach your child to feel and act helplessly. Although you prove that you hold the power, your behavior does nothing to prepare your child for the world. Such tactics produce children who either become helpless and fearful throughout life, or who grow up to become perpetrators who try to force others to do things against their will.

**Do not make any threats on which you can't or won't follow through.**
Saying that you'll leave the child at the store if she doesn't come right now is not an option. You can't abandon your child. Threatening to give your child's toys away is probably not something you'll do, so don't say you will.

However, feeling like making such threats is not an abnormal way to express your frustration. If you do make such a threat, confess to your child, saying, "I was very frustrated with your behavior (not with you) yesterday. I threatened to take all your toys away. That was not a good idea. We have to find another way for you to learn appropriate behavior." Although your child won't fully understand what you say, she'll get a sense that you care and that you seek new ways to live peacefully together.

**Do not overkill with your threats.**
Overkill is threatening to cancel a child's birthday party because she won't get dressed in a timely manner or because she won't wear what you want. Not only have you not understood what lies behind your child's stubbornness, you have used a steam shovel to dig a two-inch hole.

Make your threats reasonable, and be sure they are associated with the event at hand. You may say to an older two-year-old, "If you don't eat your breakfast now, I'll put it away and you'll have to go without." For a young two-year-old say, "If you don't stop banging with your spoon, I'll have to take the spoon away."

# Three to Four Years:

## Competence

 Once your child trusts that his needs will be met, and once he feels safe enough to separate from you and discover his own identity, your child is ready for the next stage of development: competence.

Unless your child is abused or neglected, by the time he is three years old, your child will naturally feel good about himself and his abilities. For the next year, your child will practice, practice, practice his skills, and reinforce his sense of competence.

To support his sense of competence, your child will want to explore, experiment, and expand his interests. Your child will want to do everything you or anyone else does, and he will believe he can do it. Even though your child's actual skills and perceptions are limited, he doesn't realize that his creations don't meet older people's standards. In fact, your child is not even interested in achieving a goal. He wants to do things to enjoy the process of doing. By doing, your child reinforces his feelings of competence.

Sometimes your child will appear to misbehave, but in this section you will see how to understand and guide unacceptable forms of exploration and experimentation.

Your child will sometimes become overwhelmed and frustrated by his limitations. In this section, you will learn how to protect your child from these negative feelings.

Finally, because reality and fantasy are not yet clear to your child, he needs your help to overcome his fears and understand his fantasies.

By helping your child successfully negotiate the various elements in this stage of development, you will help him become a well-rounded, creative, and capable person.

# Exploring

## Your Child's Behavior

By the time your child is about three years old, you may find it difficult to keep up with her. Just when you think you know where your
child is and what she's doing, you may realize that she's nowhere to
be found. Maybe she's gone next door because she saw the neighbors gardening. Or maybe she's gone into your bathroom to play
with your makeup, even though you told her not to.

You may feel like your three-year-old is getting into everything!

## What Your Child May Be Thinking or Feeling

The world is a wonderful place, and I love to explore it. I'm old
enough now to go off by myself. I know my neighbor's yard, and I
want to look into every nook and cranny. My neighbor lets me help
her. I can do anything—even dig a good hole to help plant flowers.

When Mommy says she wants to take me somewhere, I'm excited.
I'm going somewhere new to explore, so I want to look my best.
That's when I like to try to wear some of Mommy's makeup. She puts
on makeup when she wants to look good. So that's what I do, too. I
like to play with her makeup. And the colors are so pretty. I know
Mommy will be proud of me when I get all the makeup on just right.

## What It Means

When your child reaches age three, you will see a major change in
behavior, emotional needs, and interests. Your child has established
her identity during the previous eighteen months, so she feels good
about herself. She now enjoys one of nature's gifts—high self-
esteem, which is based on her independence and sense of identity.
Your child feels like she can do anything—she's that confident.

Your child will explore nonstop and get into things, even forbid-
den things. It's not that your child is obstinate. Your child just feels
so different, that the rules that once applied to the "little kid"—the
one she was at two—don't seem to apply anymore. Your child now
feels she can have more privileges, because she is so capable.

Your child is also unafraid to explore familiar places, such as the neighbor's yard, usual shopping areas, parks, and entertainment centers. Your child is more likely to wander off than previously, but this is a different kind of wandering than at two. Your child is not trying to separate from you. She's simply exploring—and loving it.

## What to Do

**Reaffirm the guidelines and limits of your child's world.**
You will have to reaffirm the guidelines you set down when your child was two, because your child probably thinks those guidelines no longer apply. Rethink what you want and what your child needs, and tell your child the new guidelines and limits. Say, "I want you to use your bathroom," and "I don't want you to play with my makeup. Ask me if you want to try something that belongs to me."

**Give your child things of her own.**
If your child gets into your makeup, give her a set of her own—it can even be your leftovers. Set a limit on your child's use of her makeup, if you like.

**Provide acceptable options from which your child can choose.**
Your child is now old enough to understand how to make choices to get what she wants, while staying within the limits you set. Be sure to have only a few limits, but follow through with the ones you set. Tell your child, "You may not play with my makeup, but I'll give you some of your own. If you still get into mine, I won't be able to let you use any at all, and you'll have to go to your room until you can control yourself."

**Introduce the words "control yourself."**
Age three is a good time to introduce the phrase "control yourself." When your child runs through the house, tell her, "Slow down. I don't want you to run in the house. I know you can control yourself." Your child will soon learn the meaning of the words.

When your child is unable to control herself, you can send her to her room. Your child, like other people, gets excited and overstimulated from time to time. Remove your child from the stimulating environment for a short time. This works wonders. It's better for your child to remove herself than for you to do it.

At first tell your child, "Go to your room for two minutes. I'll call you when the time is up." Do call on time. After your child learns this process, you can tell her, "Go to your room until you can control yourself." It is not uncommon for a child to go to her room, shut the door, and immediately open it again to come out. Because your child has learned the process, often that short time span is enough to quiet her down. If it isn't, send her back; only this time revert to the earlier plan, which is, "Go to your room for five minutes. I know you'll be under control by then." You temporarily take more control, until your child can gain the control by herself.

**Begin to teach your child about the dangers of the world.**
Although you don't want to scare your child, you do have to teach her to assess people. You can talk to her about different kinds of people. Say, "Some people have feelings that get out of control, and they hurt other people. You can't tell by looking at them, so you must get to know someone before you do what they say."

Be specific: "Aunt Ada, Grandma and Grandpa, Mr. Jones next door, Daddy, and I have our feelings under control, so it is safe to go with us or do what we say. Don't go with someone you don't know. We must find out if they have their feelings under control."

**Set limits on wandering.**
When you take your child out in public, even to familiar places, say, "Keep close to me. I must know where you are. If you want to explore, tell me so I know where you are." Then, the next time you are out, say, "I'm looking at dresses here. Why don't you look around in the dress department. You don't have to stay right next to me, but stay on this side of the aisle." Show your child the limits.

At three, your child doesn't have to challenge you and will probably be content to stay within the space you've defined. Be clear with your limits, though, showing your child where the floor in the department store changes color, or where there is a wide aisle, like a street, that she is not to cross.

**Follow through on consequences if your child gets into things you've labeled off limits.**
When you teach your child limits that are important to you, such

as, "You may not play with the computer," and she continues to bang on the keys, you must tell her, "You know what the rules are. You may not type on the computer. You must get down right now and go to your room for five minutes to remind you not to do that."

**Give your child child-sized opportunities to act like an adult.** Whenever possible, give your child the opportunity to mimic adult actions. Give your child her own makeup or set of tools so she can do as you do. This gives your child the opportunity to feel competent.

## What Not to Do

**Do not overly inhibit your child's explorations.** Since this is a time of great learning for your child, allow her to explore as much as possible. Set limits in terms of safety and values. Naturally, you don't want your child to play with the thermostat, which she could break or cause you to have exorbitant heating or cooling bills. And if you don't want your child to visit the neighbors unless she calls them first, teach her how to call to ask permission to visit.

**Do not punish your child for exploring.** Punishment doesn't teach your child how and within what limits to function. Your job is to provide your child with appropriate opportunities to explore. So set your limits: tell your child what she can and cannot do.

**Do not frighten your child unduly.** Preparing your child for the real world is a mammoth task. Fearing for your child's safety can lead you to use scare tactics to try to protect her. However, such tactics can create a child who is anxious in situations that are not dangerous. And throughout life, your child will tend to be unduly inhibited.

Instead, teach your child to check out situations with you, so she can learn which are safe and which are not. Tell your child, "My job is to help you learn when and where you are safe. You'll learn before long, but for now I will help you. You must tell me when you want to go somewhere, so I can check out the place with you. If you don't, then you'll have to hold my hand."

# Experimenting

## Your Child's Behavior

You may find that your three-year-old tries to accomplish things that he never tried before. He may try to write with a pen, the way his big brother writes. He may try to sweep the floor, the way Mommy and Daddy sweep. Or, he may try to make a cake by pouring flour into a big bowl and tipping the milk carton until some milk spills into the bowl. When you ask your child what he plans to put in the cake, so his efforts will result in an edible cake, he doesn't seem to care.

At the dinner table, your child may play with his food, mixing potatoes with Jell-O and diluting his creation with milk. While playing, he is probably very pleased with himself and completely absorbed in his experiment.

You may start to feel as though your child will try anything, even things that you are absolutely certain he cannot accomplish—at least not without making an enormous mess.

## What Your Child May Be Thinking or Feeling

I love doing things that Mommy and Daddy like to do—and I do them great. I bet I can even make a cake just like Mommy does. All I have to do is get some white stuff out, put it in a big bowl, and stir, stir, stir. I can do that!

Mommy tries to tell me what goes into a cake, but I don't need her to tell me. I know what makes a cake: stirring. I'm so proud of how well I do things.

Now that I'm three years old, I like food a lot. I can do all kinds of things with it. I really like to make pictures. I especially like it when we have red Jell-O because it looks great with potatoes. I know my colors now, so I know which foods to mix together. Sometimes I like to pour some of my milk onto my plate, too. The milk makes my pictures nice and juicy.

## What It Means

Your three-year-old's urge to experiment will lead him to make messes of all kinds, but his purpose is not solely to make a mess. Your child's intent is to experiment, so he can figure out how things work, how they feel, and what he can do to them.

Your child has absolutely no interest in doing things "right," because he is not heading toward a goal. That's an adult outcome. Your child's intent is to be involved in the process of doing. When your child gets tired of doing or he has learned all he wants to learn from his experiment, he'll stop. It doesn't matter whether he's finished the job by your standards.

To a three-year-old, smushing is an important skill to develop. It feels good. Your child learns about materials that way—even if the materials are mashed potatoes—and creates designs with them.

Your child probably loves color now and can recognize and name some. He likes to see how colors mix, and what better medium than food? After all, food is plentiful and readily available. Besides, food comes in a wide range of consistencies—perfect for experimentation.

Time spent "messing" now will help your child learn to think of himself as someone who can create things. Unafraid of making mistakes, your child will continue to be motivated to try new things. Since a specific goal is not of interest to him, your child is unrestricted in his thinking and doing—the ingredients of creativity.

The biggest danger of this period is trying to direct your child's behavior into "acceptable" channels. Teaching your child that there is a right way to do things restricts your child's creativity. He can learn certain ways to do things later. Then, rather than thinking of them as right, your child will simply think of them as alternatives or differences. During this period, you lay the groundwork for the way in which your child looks at and relates to the world. What you must do is help your child feel that he is a competent person who has as good a chance as the next person to succeed at anything that interests him.

## What to Do

**Provide your child with opportunities to experiment.**
Your child needs plenty of opportunities to experiment. Set up a play area where your child can glue, smush, put puzzles together, color, hammer, and do all kinds of activities. Child-proof the area so your child doesn't get into trouble by hurting himself or his work surfaces.

**Comment on your child's capability.**
Focus your remarks on what your child does, not on the end result. You may say, "You sure know how to mix those colors," or "What a fine hammering job you are doing."

**Set limits for your child by providing alternatives.**
When your child smushes his food at the dinner table, say, "The dinner table is not the place to play with your food, but I will set you up with some leftover mashed potatoes and Jell-O after dinner. You can make pictures with them while I do the dishes." Or you may prefer to substitute finger paints for food.

If your child continues to play with his food at the table, say, "If you continue to play with your food, you will have to leave the table and miss some playtime later. You may not play with your food at the table."

Consider that your child may not be hungry. At this age, doing things is often more interesting than eating. So suggest he use his words to tell you when he is not hungry. Remind your child that as soon as everyone is done eating, you will set up his special place to play. Then offer your child the opportunity to leave the table if he is not hungry. Tell him, "Under no conditions may you play with your food at the table."

## What Not to Do

**Do not evaluate your child's work.**
Under no circumstances should you evaluate your child's work, judging it as either good or bad. Even when you say, "You painted a good picture," you have set up the potential for your child to paint a "bad" picture. Keep your remarks judgment-free, and focus on the process of your child's creativity.

**Do not criticize your child's work.**
Although your child feels as though he can do anything, he, of course, cannot. His work will leave a lot to be desired by adult standards. Remember, your child is not working toward a goal. He's only interested in what and how he works. Be sure to not criticize how he does things. Your child's skills are primitive, and he will need time to become adept. Don't discourage him now.

**Do not overly restrict your child at this time.**
Because competence is at issue here, do all you can to provide your child with freedom to experiment. Restricting your child's behavior inhibits his ability to develop competence. That doesn't mean, however, your should allow him to destroy or damage things. Simply guide your child into areas where he can experiment safely and appropriately. The perfectly kept house is a detriment to your child's development at this stage. Consider the end goal before restricting your child's experimentation.

# Wanting to Help

## Your Child's Behavior

"I can do it!" may be one of your three-year-old's favorite sentences. Sometimes, you may feel that you hear it a hundred times a day. Your child may want to help you make the bed, wash the clothes, put the mail into the mail box, push the elevator buttons, wash herself, buckle her seat belt—even change the oil in the car, if she's seen you do that.

You may not think your child is old enough to do these things, but she probably thinks she is. If your child tries to accomplish something that really is too difficult for her, she may struggle with it for a bit, but she can probably accomplish more than you think.

You may enjoy the fact that your child is gaining confidence and believes she can accomplish so much. But you may also be frustrated by the delays her "help" causes. For example, if your child insists on dressing herself, it may take everyone longer to leave the house in the morning. And making dinner can sometimes become a real ordeal with your "helper" underfoot.

## What Your Child May Be Thinking or Feeling

I can do anything, and I like to tell Mommy or Daddy or anyone else who will listen. They keep trying to make me hurry, though. They forget to let me do everything by myself. I can do things for me and for them, too. I can do things just as well as they can!

Sometimes I get scared that Mommy and Daddy won't let me do everything that I can do. A lot of times they are in a hurry, and they think I'm slow. They call it "dawdling." I don't know what that is, but I don't think it's very good.

Sometimes someone tells me I did something the wrong way, even though I know I did it the right way. One time, I set the table, and a friend of Mommy's who was at the house told me I did it wrong. I put out the fork, the knife, and the spoon, but she said I didn't do it right. Now I feel a little bit scared to try to set the table again, even though I know I did it right.

## What It Means

Developing and maintaining your child's sense of competence is your primary task during this developmental period. From this feeling of competence, your child develops the motivation to try to do anything in which she's interested. The drive to try, try, try is extremely strong within her right now.

Because your child's actual perception of results is poor, she doesn't care how the outcome looks. When your child put silverware on the table, she is satisfied because she did it. When someone corrects her, she becomes crestfallen. Her goal, unlike that of grownups, is to do the job—that's all.

When an adult criticizes your child for doing something wrong, the adult plants a seed of doubt in your child about her competence. The closer the adult is to your child emotionally, the greater the doubt. Remember, your child still depends on you, so she depends on your judgment and approval.

Your child doesn't mean to dawdle during this stage. At age four, your child's intent is not to oppose you. Rather, your child becomes absorbed in what she is doing, and she wants to do everything she sees. You'd be amazed at how many new things your child sees in her world every day.

Your child doesn't intend to slow you down or get in your way: she only wants to help. She is constantly learning by "hanging out" with you. Take as much of your child's help as you can, then set a limit, having her play by herself for a while so you can meet some of your goals for the day.

Many parents find preschool programs quite useful at this time, even if you are staying home to take care of your child. The insatiable curiosity of a three-year-old challenges any parent. In lieu of extended families and neighborhood co-ops, a quality preschool program can help your child and you. Coming back together with your child at the end of the day is more sweet because of your time apart. Besides, you get time to accomplish some things. You need quiet time, too.

## What to Do

**Let your child help herself as much as possible.**
Look for ways to let your child provide for herself. Have a child-sized pitcher so your child can pour her own beverages without trying to manage a gallon jug. Allow extra time for some chores so your child can help you in the process.

**Allow your child to try a lot of things.**
Remember that reaching a goal is not the objective. Your child needs to experience the process of doing, so let her do as much as possible. Your child will likely be satisfied after tackling the task for a short while, and she will probably want to stop before the job is done.

**Set some limits on how much your child does in a day.**
You don't have to let your child control the flow of activities in your home. Rather, select certain areas and specific times when you accept her help. Other times say, "Right now I have to finish what I'm doing, but you can help me in twenty minutes." Then suggest something for your child to do while she waits for you.

Your child doesn't have to do everything all the time. Select a few things a day and tell her, "Today is your day to help with the laundry. Tomorrow you can help me cook."

**Establish a regular routine if you have to be punctual.**
Your child will do much better with a regular routine. Every morning you can go through the same steps, which will cut down on dawdling. Have clear limits. For example, serve breakfast at 7:40 in the morning, and clear the table twenty minutes later, at 8:00. If your child misses breakfast, she'll have to wait until lunch to eat—and, no, she won't starve.

## What Not to Do

**Do not let yourself become stressed by your child's needs.**
Your child loves working with someone, but you will end up doing most of the real work and she'll end up making more work for you. Although you do want to encourage your child, don't go beyond your own ability to accept her help. You can say, "Honey, your help

is valuable to me, but today I'm very busy and I have to do some things alone."

Try to find something constructive for your child to do by herself so she won't be in your way. One idea is to have your child do a project nearby. For example, if you're making dinner, you could have your child break bread crumbs into a dish—you can use the bread later to make bread pudding or feed the birds.

**Do not make your child finish her jobs.**
Your child will learn to complete a job during the next two stages of her growth. Now is not the time to try to teach her to finish. Rather, allow her to work on a project as long, or as short, as she likes. Your child will continue as long as she learns something from the process of doing.

**Do not be critical, or even concerned, about the quality of your child's work.**
Your adult perceptions will lead you to want to correct your child's work and the way in which she completes it. But your criticism or corrections will only block your child's willingness to experiment and create.

# Expanding Interests

## Your Child's Behavior

While your child's favorite statement may be, "I can do it," his favorite question may be, "Why?" You're probably hearing that a lot these days, as in, "Why do I have to brush my teeth?" "Why can't I take my teeth out like Grandpa does?" You may hear these and many, many other questions, daily.

Chances are, when you take time to answer your child's questions, he really listens, eager to learn all he can about the world around him. Your child may ask questions about animals, family members, the sky, the earth, or a picture he saw in a book three days ago.

You may be tired of all the questions, and exhausted from trying to answer them, but your child is probably working hard to figure out how all the things in his world fit together.

## What Your Child May Be Thinking or Feeling

When I look around these days, I see everything! I wonder how all these things work. I can talk really well now, so I ask lots of questions to get the answers I need. I love it when someone answers my questions. Every time I get an answer, I think of a new question. This is a great game—and I love it.

Now that I am three years old, I know just what I like and what I don't like. So if someone wants me to do something that I don't like, I ask them why I have to do that. For example, why do I have to eat lunch right now if I would rather play outside and I'm not even hungry anyway? Why does Mommy want to wash Bear in the washing machine when he is alive and should be washed in the tub like me? And why do I have to empty the dirt out of my shoes before I come into the house? Why doesn't Mommy like dirt? I do.

## What It Means

At age three, your child has become familiar enough with his environment to ask many questions. He no longer has to spend all his time coping with it, so he can expand his horizons to truly get to know what his world is about. Your child is curious.

With improving communication skills, your child will ask a million questions, often in a series. Why does it rain? What are clouds made of? How does the water get in clouds? How does the water squeeze out of the clouds? How fast does it fall? Does it get hurt when it hits the ground? And so on and so on. Each answer you give is likely to be followed by another question. Get ready.

Your child uses questions to gain information that builds a body of knowledge from which he learns. Questions also give your child a feeling of control in his life. Your child needs control because he doesn't know what to do about all the new things he sees. Questions help your child get a handle on what he sees so he doesn't feel so afraid.

At this stage, your child's imagination also bursts forth, expanding his world even more. Although sometimes afraid of what he fantasizes, your child still wants to take control of the situations in his life. That's why your child no longer asks if he can do things. He simply does them.

By taking control of what he does in a positive way, your child manages to control his fears as well as satisfy his curiosities. Your child's assertiveness is not intended to be a rebellion, nor is it aimed against you. Your child just wants to have an effect on his world.

Part of the development of your child's imagination includes having imaginary friends and giving human characteristics to his stuffed toys. Your child truly experiences these "friends" as real, because he has not yet sorted reality from fantasy, as adults do.

## What to Do

**Answer as many of your child's questions as possible.**
Although your child will likely ask more questions in a day than you wish to answer, respond as often as you can. By answering your child's questions, you not only help your child gather much-needed information about the world, but you also reinforce his curiosity. Thanks to your efforts, your child will develop a high motivation for learning that will last the rest of his life.

Your child is not yet using the questioning process to put off doing something. He really wants to know. As he gathers information, your child expands his view of the world.

**Allow your child to expand his horizons.**
Realize that your child is getting older and is ready to expand his range of responsibility. He wants to be more in control of his actions. Your child has to expand his horizons physically, mentally, socially, and emotionally.

**Let your child tell you what he plans to do.**
Your child is not trying to "get away with" something at this stage. Rather, he's trying to further develop his sense of competence. To do that, your child must expand what he does and be more in charge of himself and his environment. Remember, your child is no longer the dependent baby of one and two.

## What Not to Do

**Do not inhibit your child's curiosity.**
Don't squelch your three-year-old's expansion by being too busy to answer questions. Let your child take charge of situations whenever possible. Of course, sometimes you have to be the one in control. When confronted with a situation about which you are unsure, stop and take the time to think about whether you need to exert leadership. Consider whether your child should be allowed the freedom to follow his own lead.

For example, your child may wish to learn how to empty wastebaskets into the trash can. Although he may spill a few pieces of paper, your child is probably capable of accomplishing this job. And, most likely, nothing will hurt him in the process. Even if he drops the garbage can lid, no real damage will occur. So let your child figure out how to empty the trash. His curiosity will be satisfied, and his sense of competence will be reinforced.

**Do not rush when answering your child's questions.**
Often, in the hurry of a busy day, your child's questions will seem to be a nuisance, getting in the way of the things you're trying to do. But take the time to answer your child's questions thoughtfully. You

have a wonderful chance to not only teach your child through your answers but to bond with him. Your child will remember that you were there for him.

**Do not take offense when your child tells you what to do.**
Your should be pleased when your child tells you what to do. When your child says, "I can't go to bed, now, I'm busy," say, "I'm glad you told me. I know how busy you are these days. Please wind things down as soon as possible." It won't be long until your child is ready to cooperate with you, and he'll want to cooperate because you've been so understanding.

Remember, your child is not rebelling. He's just absorbed in what he's doing.

# "Misbehaving"

## Your Child's Behavior

Even if your child has been very easy-going, you may have some difficulties with her when she reaches the age of three. For example, if you take your usually well-behaved child to your haircut appointment, thinking she will play quietly by your chair, your child may walk away and examine the hair-setting supplies near someone else's chair. Or she may take a pen out of your purse and draw a picture—on the floor.

If you discuss this behavior with your child, she may not understand why you think she did anything wrong, and that may make you might feel even more frustrated. You may wonder whether you'll ever convince your child to behave according to your rules.

## What Your Child May Be Thinking or Feeling

I love to explore new things. When Mommy takes me someplace new, I like to see everything there is to see. If Mommy walks around, she usually stops me when I start to explore. But if she sits and can't get up right away to come after me, I have a much better time. That's when I really have a chance to see all the new things around me.

This place has so many things I've never seen before. I have to find out about each of them. This shiny floor would look even prettier with a picture. I think I will draw one with the pretty, shiny pencil I saw in Mommy's bag. I always know that Mommy will be proud of what I do, because I'm such a big girl now. Sometimes, though, she is not happy with what I do, but I don't know why she becomes angry.

## What It Means

The idea of a misbehaving child is an adult notion. Children don't set out to misbehave. They are doing something that interests them when they cross the line of "good" behavior. As a result, adults apply the label of "misbehavior," but that is never the intent of your child, especially at three.

If your child is totally curious at this age and feels safe enough to "misbehave," you've actually done a lot of things right. By creating an environment in which your child feels comfortable and safe, you invite your child to look around for something new to explore. If your child was less comfortable, she would cling to you and to everything that's familiar. Then she would not get into trouble.

By not fully understanding the curious nature of the secure child, parents sometimes forget to check out their child's environment. Childproofing will save you from many uncomfortable situations. Any lively three-year-old would be drawn to the beauty shop's carts full of strange and wonderful things.

At this age, your child is not yet sure what is within her limits and what is outside her limits. A shiny floor seems a perfectly natural surface upon which to draw. After all, if the child doesn't have paper, what else is she supposed to use? You just have to think like a child to understand this: shiny pencils and shiny floors go together.

At this stage, your child's intent is not to embarrass you, or hurt you, or do anything else to you, nor does she mean to thwart you or rebel against you. Your child is simply exploring.

Although most parents respond to their child's inappropriate exploration with embarrassment and anger, you must realize that you and your child are not one and the same. Sure, you are responsible, to a degree, for what your child does and doesn't do, but you cannot be so vigilant that your child never gets into something she should not. Remember, your child will learn much more from her mistakes than she will from you overcontrolling her actions so she never makes a mistake.

## What to Do

**Check out new environments.**
When you take your child to a new place, always check out the place. Keep a watchful eye for things that would be new to your child, especially things she can pick up, handle, or take apart.

When your child takes her brother's model airplane apart, remember that three-year-olds are curious and like to take everything apart. So check to discover what may fall victim to your child's curiosity. Then you can set limits for your child to follow.

**Show your child what is okay to explore.**
Often people don't mind letting your child explore in a new arena, but you must gain their permission first—to protect another person's property, your reputation, and your child.

You may discover that the shopkeeper has some old supplies in the back with which your child can play. If not, then explain to your child that the supplies are off limits, "hands off," and show her what she *can* do.

**Set limits to protect other's property.**
Just as you have done at home with family members' property, you must set "hands off" limits on others' property outside the home. Your child may see someone handle an object and not realize why she isn't allowed to handle the same object. A three-year-old doesn't know much about ownership. She must learn.

**Teach your child to ask permission to touch new things.**
When your child is three, teach her to come to you to ask permission to look at and touch objects that are new to her. Remind your child of this rule by saying, "Remember this shop belongs to Ms. Smith. Everything in it is hers. Ask me if you want to touch something that doesn't belong to you."

Later, after your child has mastered this lesson, she can ask for permission directly, but that is likely to be at age four or five. Right now, you are your child's conduit to permission.

**Help your child fix any messes she makes.**
Since your child is learning what is and is not appropriate for her to touch and do, your main focus is to teach her those differences. Remember, your child is not rebelling against you or being obstinate. She's learning. So help your child when she makes a mistake. However, don't do the whole job yourself. Include your child in the cleanup or fix-up. That's part of her lesson.

**Deal with your own feelings about what happened.**
Getting embarrassed and feeling angry because your child made a mistake is natural, but don't take your feelings out on your child.

First, decide how to fix the current situation. Focus on solutions. Observe what's happened and decide if any actual damage occurred. Beauty supplies on the floor look bad, but no permanent damage actually occurred.

On the other hand, a pen marking did temporarily damage the floor, but it can be removed. Assess the real damage, and share your evaluation with your child as you go through the mental process. Then you turn the situation into a teaching opportunity. Speak in a matter-of-fact way. Study the situation so you can make adjustments the next time you enter a situation that's new to your child.

## What Not to Do

**Do not punish your child.**
Punishment serves no purpose other than to relieve you. Although I empathize with your feelings, you, as the adult, can learn to manage your feelings rather than take them out on your child. Teach instead.

**Do not stop taking your child to public places.**
Although you may have stopped taking your child to crowded public places when she was two, you don't have to do this now—if you use a bit of judgment.

Your child still needs supervision, so decide whether you will be free to give it. Or consider whether someone else can provide the necessary supervision. Your child is probably quite able to sit with you in a restaurant because you are right there, but she is probably not ready to be left completely alone anywhere for a period of time. She's still too curious and too inexperienced. Find a happy medium.

**Do not think you are a bad parent because your child misbehaves.**
Just because your child sometimes gets into things, don't automatically jump to the conclusion that you are an inadequate or bad parent. Check whether you are providing the guidelines, limits, and supervision your child needs at this time. Figure out ways to include your child in various trips and activities while protecting her and others from her curiosity. But forgive yourself if sometimes your child-proofing proves less than adequate. Remember, your child is healthy and secure if she explores.

# Feeling Fearful

## Your Child's Behavior

Children of this age commonly believe in monsters and are afraid of them. Your child may tell you a monster is hiding in his closet, one that only comes out at night when you're not in the room. Your child may try to clean his closet during the day to get rid of the monsters. Or he may fight you when bedtime comes around because he's afraid of the monsters, which, he says, come out when you turn off the light.

Your child may also resist any change in his life. For example, if you try to rearrange the furniture in your child's room, he may cry or yell. If you buy your child new slippers, he may insist on wearing the old ones. Because of such behavior, you may think your child is stuck in a rut—clinging tightly to his clothes, toys, and anything else that is familiar to him. And, although he may enjoy playing with new friends, your child may not want to change any of his routines. If the family does something new, your child may seem anxious. He may watch scary movies with you or his older siblings, but then he may become scared and resist going to bed at bedtime.

Your child may act as though he wants to explore everything new he sees, and, at the same time, not do anything new at all. Your child may seem to be very cautious and very inquisitive at the same time, and that behavior is probably very confusing to you.

## What Your Child May Be Thinking or Feeling

These days, I feel afraid of a lot of things. I hear strange noises and see funny-looking shadows everywhere. I feel weird, scary feelings a lot. They get worse at night. Then I can't tell what's real and what's not.

Mommy says it's my imagination, but I don't know. What I feel is real to me. I don't want to go to bed now or be in the dark. I don't like anything to change because then I have to get used to what's new—and that frightens me. I want my old slippers and my old toys. And I want everything in my life to stay the same as it has always been.

I like to play with my big brother and sister. They're big and strong, and I love them. They protect me. They tell me there are no such things as monsters, and that I shouldn't be afraid, but I don't know. I do know that I can't sleep very well after I watch scary movies with them. I wish I could get them to do something else with me, so I could still be with them, but not see all that scary stuff.

## What It Means

Curiosity drives your child to take in more information than ever before. Cognitively, your child cannot yet separate reality from fantasy. Trying to make sense of all the new experiences takes time.

But without previous experience to tell him what is dangerous and what is safe, your child feels apprehensive. He doesn't know the meaning of what he sees, hears, and senses. That leaves your child feeling helpless and vulnerable. Your child's vivid imagination fills in the gaps. When his imagination takes over, it supplies your child with all kinds of thoughts, some of which are scary, about what he hears, sees, and feels.

Although much more independent than he was at two, your child doesn't have the skills to be on his own yet. And he doesn't really feel ready to leave you and explore very far. That will come at age four. Your child's curiosity already stretches him as much as he can stand, so he likes to have everything around him stable.

Going to bed at night, being in darkness, and spending time in strange environments heightens your child's fears. The resistance you encounter is not against you—it's your child's reaction to feeling afraid and helpless. Your job is to reassure your child, change as little as possible in his life, and help him feel safe.

## What to Do

**Explain to your child the meaning of imagination.**
Talk to your three-year-old about dreams. Say, "Do you see pictures in your mind? Tell me about them."

When he does, introduce the word "imagination." Your child can learn to use that word to describe any pictures, feelings, or words that his mind creates.

**Share your imagination.**
Say, "I have pictures, too. Sometimes when I hear a sound and I don't know what it is, my imagination makes a picture in my mind. Sometimes the picture is a happy one; sometimes it's a scary one." Then say, "Do you ever get scary pictures in your mind?"
Sharing your experience helps your child share his.

**Make up imaginary stories together.**
Your child will feel more secure when you make up imaginary stories together. You may want to make up a story about your child's favorite animal. Say, "Once upon a time a hippopotamus went for a walk." Then turn to your child and say, "Where do you think the hippopotamus wanted to walk?" By asking your child leading questions, you help him create a story. When you finish, you can say, "We sure made up a good story together. We both have good imaginations."

**Reassure your child about monsters.**
When your child is afraid a monster is under his bed or in his closet, reassure him, saying, "I've never seen a monster in the closet. I don't believe one lives there."
If your child counters, saying, "Yes, he does. I know there's a monster under the bed," say, "Then let's look together. I'll help you check under your bed. Would you like me to look first?" You could even get a broom and sweep under the bed.

**Provide your child with ways to feel safe and secure.**
Be sure to have a night-light for your child. If your child wants his bedroom door open, let him have it that way. Have your child sleep with a stuffed animal that is assigned to protect him. You can even specially assign a stuffed animal the task of keeping any and all monsters in check. Then place that animal in the closet door or under the bed, giving it direct orders. Say, "Now you be sure to keep all monsters out of here, so Willie can go to sleep."
Some three-year-olds like to set up or build a snug tent in which to sleep. You can also place a blanket over a card table if you don't have a tent handy. Remember, this period only lasts for a few months.

**Encourage your child to protect himself.**
Encourage your child to protect himself so he feels he has some power over scary things. You may want to share feelings you had at his age. Say, "When I was three, I worried about a monster living in my closet. My daddy told me to make a big noise to scare it away."

Then ask, "Do you know what?"

When your child says, "What?" respond with, "It worked. No monster ever came near me again. You can do that, too."

Teaching your child to protect himself helps him build feelings of security that will turn into feelings of powerfulness when he becomes four, and into feelings of courageousness when he is an adult. Frightened adults didn't learn to protect themselves or were forced prematurely to fake courage.

**Keep your child on schedule.**
Even though going to bed is scary, keep your child on as regular a schedule as possible. Be matter-of-fact, use the protections you have agreed upon, and say, "No more getting up. It's time to go to sleep." Your schedule also serves as protection.

**Protect your child from teasing.**
Protect your child from being taken advantage of during this period. Sometimes older children and even adults don't understand how vulnerable children can feel at this stage. The scars from teasing can last a lifetime. Don't allow teasing.

## What Not to Do

**Do not make fun of your frightened child.**
Never tease, make fun of, or discount your child's fears. Don't say, "You're a sissy," or put a child down because he is afraid.

Respect your child's feelings of fear and help him overcome them. You can say, "I can see you are afraid of monsters. I don't believe in them, but let's look under the bed together. I'll help you. Would you like a flashlight in your bed so you can turn it on any time you want?" Giving your child the power to turn on the light helps him feel more able to stay in control.

**Do not argue about the reality of monsters.**
Sure, you know monsters aren't real, but don't argue with your child. That only serves to make your child feel more helpless and intimidated, not just by the monster he feels is real, but also by you. Simply say in a matter-of-fact voice that you don't believe monsters exist. "I have learned since I was your age that monsters don't really exist, but I sure thought they did then—just like you."

By sharing your early experience, you give your child someone with whom to identify. When you argue, you separate yourself from your child, and he feels alone with his fears.

**Do not overprotect your child.**
Don't collapse your limits because your child is afraid. Don't let your child stay up extremely late or sleep with you because he fears monsters or imaginary beings. (If your child has suffered an actual trauma, this doesn't apply. Then you want to provide more protection.)

Don't talk a lot about your child's fears to him or others. Know that this is a normal part of a three-year-old's development and will pass naturally. Simply provide temporary support, which includes keeping limits and rules, such as bedtime, in place.

**Do not force your child into new and strange situations.**
This is not the time to introduce your child to spook houses, scary movies, or staying overnight at strange houses. Some children of this age are even afraid of Halloween costumes. Respect your child's fears and wait a year or two. Your child will probably love the "scariness" by then.

# Feeling Overwhelmed and Frustrated

## Your Child's Behavior

There may be days when your child whines for hours at a time. She may start having temper tantrums at this age, throwing herself on the floor, kicking, screaming, and crying for no reason—at least no reason you can see. Your child may interrupt you constantly when you're on the telephone, to the extent that you wonder whether you'll ever be able to finish a conversation again.

In fact, you may feel that your child is easy to be with one moment and very difficult to tolerate the next. She may act like a "big girl" one minute and a helpless baby the next.

## What Your Child May Be Thinking or Feeling

There is so much for me to do these days—so many things I have to do. A lot of those things I do all by myself. I get up, get dressed, eat, brush my teeth, decide what to play with, help Mommy take care of my little brother, play with him, find paper to draw on, try to get my markers to work, find something interesting to do . . . and I have to do all of this myself!

Sometimes I feel as though I have too much to do. Sometimes I want to quit. I know I'm a big girl and I try to do a lot, but sometimes it feels like too much. Sometimes I wish I was a baby again, and Mommy could take care of me the way she takes care of my baby brother.

When I feel like I have too much to do, I go outside to play. I run and jump very, very hard, and then I feel better. But then sometimes I get very thirsty, so I ask Mommy to get me a drink. I know she's busy and I could get it myself, but I'm so tired. I need her to take care of me. When she does, I feel better. She makes everything all right.

Even though I'm a big girl now, I still have to make sure Mommy is there for me. Sometimes when she is on the telephone, I get scared. She pays attention to someone else instead of me. What if I need her and she isn't there for me? I'd better check to make sure she's still there for me. I say, "Mommy, Mommy," but she still talks to the other person, so I have to say it again. "Mommy, Mommy." Now she puts the phone down and turns to see me, but she doesn't have a happy look on her face. She looks very angry. I wonder why. Maybe she's mad at the person on the phone.

## What It Means

Your child is going through an in-between age—she is not a baby anymore, and she's not yet fully independent, either. One minute your child feels very capable and able to do many things for herself; the next she feels overwhelmed and frustrated.

Your child works very hard at this age. She's curious, wants to try everything, and gets very tired from all the activity. She has no idea how to moderate her level of activity, so she throws herself into whatever she is doing and, consequently, exhausts herself.

The more your child exhausts herself, the more likely she is to just give up, throw herself on the floor in frustration, wail with helplessness, sniffle over the loss of her competence, and, finally, suck her thumb like she did when she was little. Your child feels more like a baby than a three-year-old at such times.

One minute your child can do all sorts of things. The next she can't even get her own juice. It's at this moment that she calls for her steadfast, always-present Mommy or Daddy, who can make things right for her.

When she does, it's a sign that you've done a whole lot right. You've created a bond between you and your child that every child needs. You've compassionately and continuously taken care of your child's needs when she couldn't care for herself. Your child trusts you.

You are very important to your child. Of course, your child will only want you when she needs you. That's what childhood is all about. Your child has to check that you'll be there for her, and check she does, especially when any signs exist that you may be unavailable, such as when you are on the telephone or talking to the neighbor.

## What to Do

**Be flexible.**
You have to be flexible if you are to stand ready to guide your child through this period. Although you may not like to be needed one minute, and cast aside the next, your have to be able to follow your child's lead. Your child's healthy growth and development depend on your flexibility and steadfastness through thick and thin.

**Only do what your child needs and wants you to do at this time.**
When your child is overwhelmed and frustrated and wants you to baby her a little, go ahead. Say, "Right now you need Mommy to help you, and I will. Soon you'll feel able to take over for yourself again." The rest of the time, allow your child to be the self-sufficient child she is becoming.

**Set firm limits on your child's self-care.**
When your child is so active that she tires herself out, insist that she rest a while. Although she may fight you, be firm. Say, "I know you don't want to lie down now, but I must insist. You don't have to sleep, just rest. We all have to learn when it's time to rest; even grownups must remember to rest."

**Teach your child how to express her needs.**
If you begin at this age to teach your child how you want her to express her needs, your efforts will pay off for years to come. If you give your child what she wants when she whines, she'll whine a lot. If you give in when your child nags, you guessed it, she'll nag and nag and nag. If you always deny your child what she wants, she'll learn to be sneaky. Tell her, "Look, my job is to help you get what you want. So, if you'll talk to me in a regular voice, I'll try to figure out some reasonable way to help you get it."

You can usually find a way to negotiate with your child so she gets what she wants, while staying within your limits. For example, if your child wants a cookie before dinner, have her select one and save it in a safe place for after dinner. Both of you win this way.

**Check your child's schedule to be sure it's not too busy.**
Because your child is able to do many things now, she may get involved in too many things too much of the time. Stop and look

at the commitments you and your child have made. See whether she has any free time.

The hurried child, even at three, is a product of the Western world. You don't have to follow suit. Childhood should be a time for play, creativity, and peace. Your child will make maximum use of her talents and potential when she grows up, even though she doesn't fill every hour of her waking day with activity now.

**Reassure your child that you are available for her at all times.**
When you are on the phone or engaged in conversation with someone else, you probably want to push your child away when she tries to interrupt. I'm sure you've noticed that such actions seem to make matters worse.

Instead of trying to shush or scold your child, take five seconds to reach out and draw her to you. You may want to excuse yourself from the phone, pull your child to you, and say, "I'm glad you came to check on me to see what I'm doing. You can stay right here if you'd like."

Although this may seem the opposite of what you want, your child will probably leave the second she is reassured that she can stay.

## What Not to Do

**Do not put your child down for acting like a baby.**
When your child is overwhelmed and frustrated, she will act as she did at a younger age. Don't point this out to her or in any way put her down for it. Even adults "act like babies" sometimes. Surely you can understand a three-year-old's need to be taken care of for what it is: a temporary need to abdicate responsibility and be cared for. Understand your child's needs. Be sure to do the same for yourself from time to time.

**Do not worry that your child will stay babyish.**
Acting younger is a temporary state of affairs, one that will pass if you don't make too big a deal of it. Don't over- or underpamper your child. Help your child as much as she needs, then let her go.

**Do not reject your child when she needs you.**
When your child needs you, be there for her. If you fear that something is wrong with your child when she acts needy, you may want to push her to behave in a grownup fashion. But this creates a situation in which your child's needs don't get met directly. Because you reject her, your child may feel ill, which requires you to care for her. She doesn't purposely get sick to make this happen, but she will feel bad, nonetheless.

By caring for your child's needs directly and compassionately, you actually help her become stronger in the long run. Your child will also know when to ask for help in the future.

# Distinguishing Fantasy and Reality

## Your Child's Behavior

Your child may have an imaginary friend; lots of children do at this age. Your child's imaginary friend is dear to him and he takes this friend seriously; the imaginary friend may eat with your child, sleep in his bed, take baths with him, have lengthy conversations with him—and you'd better not sit on one in the car.

Your child may even want, or expect, you to help care for this imaginary friend. Your child may want you to leave out a bath towel for his friend, or provide food for him, or move your bags over in the car so he has enough room. Sometimes your child may tell you where the imaginary friend is and what he's doing. But at other times, your child may act very hurt if you don't already know where his friend is sitting and see exactly what he needs.

## What Your Child May Be Thinking or Feeling

I have a new friend who is with me all the time. His name is Sam. Daddy put his papers and bags right on top of Sam in the car today. I don't know why he did that. He should be nicer to Sam.

Sam is my very best friend. He knows everything I think. He feels the same way I do. He likes what I like, and he wants what I want. We go everywhere together.

Even though I have a baby sister, I sometimes get lonely. My sister can't do much yet except lie around and eat and sleep and cry. Since Sam came, I don't feel alone anymore. I have someone to play with all the time. I like that.

I don't understand grownups. They don't understand how the world works. They don't treat Sam very nicely. It's not that they hurt him—except when they sit on him. It's just that they don't think about what he needs. They forget to leave a place for him to sit in the car, and they don't remember to set him a place at the table for dinner. I always have to do that myself. But I know how to do that, and I always take good care of my friend.

## What It Means

An imaginary friend acts as a safety valve for all the overwhelming pressures of being a three-year-old. Your child is too inexperienced to cope with everything that happens in his world. Remember how curious three-year-olds are. Although your child's brain is developing quickly, your child still has too much to process and understand.

Your child's imaginary friend, or friends—some children have several—are a perfectly normal coping mechanism that may stay around for as long as a year, or even longer. Nothing is wrong with your child. Rather, his creativity has conjured up a solution to help him get his needs met.

The mind of a three-year-old thinks in a very concrete way, often putting facts and conclusions together in an order that is logical to the child, but not to adults. For example, your child may think that fire trucks start fires, because every time he sees a fire truck, he also sees a fire. Your child's thinking will get straightened out with experience. Trying to talk logic at this time is pointless. Instead, listen and you'll discover how your child's mind works. It will help you understand him.

Because your child puts facts and reality together in strange ways, an imaginary friend can be an asset to any child of this age. You will hear your child talk to his friend. If you listen to the conversations without interrupting, you'll discover that your child is trying to work through what he sees and feels in relation to the world around him. It's his way to figure out life.

Your child lives daily with his fantasy companion and expects you to respect him. You must. Remember, in addition to sorting out his world, your child is also expanding his care for others while he practices the development of friendship and empathy with a "friend" who accepts him unconditionally.

## What to Do

**Respect your child's imaginary friend(s).**
Treat your child's imaginary friend(s) the same way you treat your child. Don't bend the rules for the imaginary friend, but respect his or her presence. Remember, your child is learning to relate to others, and his social and empathy skills are growing. Respect and admire the friendships your child is developing, and he will learn an early lesson in caring for others that will transfer to real people later.

**Consider an imaginary friend as an opportunity for practice.**
All the lessons you want to teach your child can be reinforced through the imaginary friend. Your child will be able to practice two-fold because of his friend. When you tell your child to brush his teeth carefully, you can also tell him to see that his friend also brushes. Say, "Be sure Sam brushes up and down and way in back." Although you just told your child to do that, you get a free opportunity to repeat your lesson without seeming to nag. What a deal!

**Explain as much as possible about how the world works.**
Children of this age want to know how everything works. Any time you can explain how something works before your child comes to his own conclusions, you have an opportunity to get the facts straight. You can sit down with models and show your child how a fire starts, how the call goes to the fire station, how the firefighters jump on the truck, and how the truck drives to the fire to put out the fire. Then you can drive to the fire station on a quiet day and have a tour.

Once your child comes to a wrong conclusion, you can try to show him the way things really work, but don't argue. Ask, "Would you like me to show you how firefighters work?" When your child says yes, go through the role-play situation. You don't have to point out that his thinking was in error. Let that go. Your child will shift his thinking on his own, and he may tell his imaginary friend about it, too.

## What Not to Do

**Do not try to talk your child out of his friend.**
If you are worried about your child having an imaginary friend, realize that many children do; it's normal. Don't try to talk your child out of believing in his friend. An imaginary friend is a coping tool that your child's mind creates. The friend serves a purpose, and your child is stronger because of the friendship.

**Do not argue with your child about reality.**
Your child doesn't learn the cognitive lessons you try to teach when you argue with him. Instead, your child experiences a power struggle between you and him. To your child, his reality is true. You can show your child the difference between your reality and his, and you can show him how you come to your perspective, but then allow your child to think for himself.

Say, "Here's how I see fires and fire trucks. First the fire starts. Here are some ways that happens." You have a good opportunity to teach some fire safety lessons.

Continue by saying, "Then the fire alarm is called in and the fire truck comes." Finally ask, "How does that sound to you? You think about it. We'll talk some more tomorrow. Would you like to go to the fire station on my first day off?"

If your child insists that fire trucks start fires, say, "I respect how you think. I think differently. That's okay. Sometimes you'll think one way, and I'll think another."

**Do not worry that your child is mentally ill.**
Childhood fantasies are normal, temporary, and disappear as soon as your child's mind catches up with all the input he experiences.

**Do not think your child is lonely because he has an imaginary friend.**
Children in big families have imaginary friends, and so do only children. Children who play alone have imaginary friends, and so do children who have a number of playmates available. Don't worry about your child. Rejoice that your child is creative, verbal, and coping well with growing up.

# Four to Five and a Half Years:
## Power

 As your child approaches age four, you will see a remarkable change. No longer will your child be as interested in helping you or showing you what she can do. No longer will your cuddly little girl want you nearby to give approval and support—at least, not nearly as much as before. Instead, you'll find that you live with a power-hungry, often-bossy, limit-pushing youngster who shows few signs of sweetness and many indications of a take-charge adult.

When these changes occur, you can be certain your child's development is right on track. She's moving into the fourth stage of development: a sense of powerfulness.

Although this stage is sometimes very demanding of parents, you will come to appreciate this stage once you understand how it works. During your child's infancy, she was dependent upon you to meet her needs. Then she began to separate from you emotionally. She discovered a lot about her identity, her sense of competence thrived as she experimented as a three-year-old, and now she's ready to meet her own needs. In just three short years, your child has grown from being dependent on you to meet her needs, to striving to meet her own needs!

To get her needs met, your child must develop feelings of emotional powerfulness. Fortunately, these come instinctively from within your child, though you can support them or weaken them.

While you support your child's development at this stage, you must set reasonable limits so your child's behavior is constructive. Just as a fire is dangerous and destructive when allowed to burn out of control, but is wonderful when contained within a fireplace or furnace, power must also be contained. You must not allow your child's powerfulness to get out of control, for your child's sake and others'.

At four, your child's attempts to develop powerfulness are awkward. Your child has not yet learned to modulate the energy. But during this twelve-to-eighteen-month period, your child will learn how to control her power, with your help and guidance. Your child will model the way you handle your power in relation to her and others.

Your child needs emotional powerfulness to develop assertiveness (rather than aggressiveness), responsibility, self-control, and good judgment. Ultimately, your child's powerful feelings help her become compassionate and protective toward others. Remember, powerfulness has to do with your child's control to get her needs met—not control over anyone else.

In this section, you will learn what to do when your child wants, even demands, to take responsibility for herself.

Once your child obtains some power, she will want to test that power and see where you limit her behavior. Your job is to support your child during her exploration, protect your child when she needs protection, and always serve as a good model for your child to appropriately handle emotional power.

You also serve an important role when your child loses power or when she becomes emotionally stressed. In this section you will discover how to handle these situations effectively, so your child learns how to build skills to help her recover from stressful situations: skills she can use throughout her lifetime.

# Discovering Power

## Your Child's Behavior

By the time your child is four years old, you may begin to feel that, occasionally, his behavior is an attempt to manipulate you.

For example, your child may choose the end of his bedtime ritual—whether that includes a bath, stories and songs, or just a simple tuck-in—as a great time to ask you lots of questions, even questions you've answered many times before. Every time you get up to walk toward the door, your child may have just one more question that he has to have answered at that exact moment.

If you've always been very patient with your child and made every effort to answer his questions, he probably knows he can count on that behavior from you at bedtime, too. Consequently, getting your four-year-old to bed can turn into a very lengthy ordeal.

## What Your Child May Be Thinking or Feeling

I am four years old now, and I don't like to be told what to do. I like to be in charge of things and do them my own way.

If I'm not tired and I don't want to go to bed, I know I can just ask Mommy or Daddy lots of questions to keep them from leaving my room. Then I don't have to go to bed until I'm ready. That way I can be in control of my own bedtime.

Sometimes I like to put a towel around my shoulders and jump off the couch with the towel flying behind me like a big cape. I feel just like Batman when I do that, and Batman is very powerful. Sometimes I yell really loudly when I do that, and that adds power, too.

I know I have the power to do anything. Mommy and Daddy better get used to me being in charge.

## What It Means

Information provides feelings of powerfulness. On top of that, if your child uses questions to avoid doing something he doesn't want to do, such as going to bed, he asserts his power over the situation. Although you may not like it, you can be glad the behavior is present.

Parents give or withhold power from their children. To raise a responsible, self-sufficient child, you must learn to give your child power. Your job is to set limits that are reasonable while you give your child as much power as possible. That way, your child can make choices within guidelines that are acceptable to you.

Your child wants to make the choice about when to go to bed. Being able to make choices supports your child's growing feelings of powerfulness, as does being in charge of his bedtime. When you and your child work together as partners—a major shift in your relationship—you teach your child to be independent and in charge of himself in acceptable ways.

Naturally attracted to superheroes at this age, your child will try to imitate their seemingly superhuman powerfulness. Girls as well as boys play superhero. Wonder Woman naturally comes to mind with girls, but they also imitate any popular hero of the moment. A cape becomes a magical source of power; one that helps your fledgling hero learn to feel powerful at a time when his experience is limited, but his desire to feel emotionally powerful is high.

## What to Do

**Support your child's desire to act powerfully.**
When your child wants to be his own boss, give him some power over himself. If he delays going to bed, you may say, "I'd like to put you in charge of your bedtime, as long as you take good care of yourself. You're responsible now, so I can trust you to do what is good for you."

**Give your child choices.**
One of the most effective ways to give children power is to offer them choices. Always offer your child choices of which you approve, so no matter what your child chooses, his choices will be okay with you. You may say, "Would you rather put your pajamas on before or after your story?" Either way, your child will be ready for bed and a story.

**Set reasonable limits on your child's behaviors.**
Let your child know how he can be powerful without getting out of control. Allow your child opportunities to act powerfully within

defined guidelines. That teaches him how to be powerful in an acceptable way. You may say, "You can decide whether you want to go to bed at 8:30 in the evening or 8:45, as long as you go to bed at the time you choose." That way your child gets the power of choice, while you make the point that he must go to bed once he's committed.

**Get your own power under control.**
You may discover during this period that you must work with your own thoughts about powerfulness. If you expect your child to jump at the snap of your fingers, then you may want to rethink what you were taught about power. Was that the way you were raised? Parents often pass on the way they were treated without thinking about the repercussions. Stop and think.

Remember, this is the power your child uses to meet his own needs, not power over someone else, including you. You, too, once needed support in the development of your power. Make this development okay for your child, whether you were given power as a child or not. Both you and your child gain.

**Play along with your child's interest in superheroes.**
Most of the superheroes are "good guys" who use their powerfulness to help others. These mythical characters teach your child how to use power on behalf of others.

While your child plays at being a superhero, he actually practices being powerful. Just be sure that the heroes your child chooses to emulate are the good guys.

## What Not to Do

**Do not be afraid of your child's power displays.**
When you've been the victim of someone else's power, wielded physically or emotionally, it is difficult to accept high levels of out-of-control powerfulness. If you were taught powerlessness as a child, you may be intimidated by powerful people, including your own child, who is not frightened the way you once were.

Since your four-year-old doesn't yet know how to handle his power, it may come out in the form of brute force. That looks frightening. Your job is to rise to the occasion and guide your child, not intimidate him or back off from him. Humor can help at times like these—say no with a twinkle in your eye. When you see your child approach another child with a gleam in his eye, and you know your child has cooked up something, intervene. Walk over to your child, lean down, and whisper near his ear, "Don't even think about doing what you're thinking of doing."

**Do not squelch your child's powerfulness.**
As a parent, you really are more powerful than your child. You can stop the development of your child's powerfulness, but doing so teaches your child to be helpless, irresponsible, bullying, or rageful. None of these is a constructive way to live: all of these leave the person out of control and destructive to himself or others.

**Do not see your child's powerfulness as against you.**
Your child's developing sense of powerfulness is not against you. It's for him. Although your child may object to doing what you want, he doesn't resist to make your life hard. Your child objects because that makes him feel powerful.

**Do not fail to enforce limits that you set.**
When you decide on limits that are constructive and useful for your child, follow through on them. Although you may be tempted to relax limits, especially when you're tired, don't do it.

When you tell your child he must stay in bed once he's committed to a time, be prepared to follow through with the consequences if he doesn't. Say, "If you don't stay in bed when you decide to go, I won't be able to let you choose tomorrow night. You'll have to go to bed at 8:30 tomorrow night." The next night, you must follow through, even if you can see a good reason to relax the limits. Maybe Grandma is visiting and she'd like to spend a little extra time with her grandchild. Normally that would be okay, but remember what you're teaching your child, and abide by the limit you set.

# Taking Power

## Your Child's Behavior

Your four-year-old child may suddenly want to be in charge of everything and do everything for herself. If your child wanted to play at a neighbor's house when she was three, for example, she may have asked for permission. But at four, she may just tell you, "I'm going next door to play with Sally. I'll be back later."

Or your child may suddenly start telling you what she will and will not eat, instead of asking what you're cooking. For example, no matter what you have planned, your child may announce that she's going to have peanut butter and jelly for dinner. And if you try to explain why she needs vegetables for dinner, your four-year-old may argue with you.

If you see your child climbing the tree in the back yard and tell her to be careful, she may laugh at you and tell you she knows exactly what she is doing and doesn't need any instructions from you.

You may feel that your child has become very stubborn and bossy and is trying to run the entire household. In fact, she just may be.

## What Your Child May Be Thinking or Feeling

I sure am big these days. I can do anything. I can even climb almost to the top of the tree. I learned how to do it by going carefully from one branch to the next. At first I was a little scared, but I had to do it. Mommy tried to keep me from climbing so high, but I knew she was wrong.

Now that I'm four, I know more than Mommy does. Mommy used to be a lot more helpful than she is now. Now she really gets in my way. She doesn't seem to understand that I know more than she does—at least, I know more about me than she does. I have to stand up for what I know and what I want.

Since I know more than Mommy does now, I don't have to ask her if I want to go somewhere. I know where I'm going, and I can just go and do what I want. Nothing will happen to me. Mommy worries too much.

## What It Means

During the last developmental stage, your child increased her competence by experimenting with all kinds of things. Now your child is experimenting with relationships and the power to do for herself. Her emphasis is on the building of emotional powerfulness.

In the beginning, your child builds her powerfulness by simply taking power. Your child asserts herself without thought for another person. Realize that your child still doesn't have compassion or empathy for others. This awareness comes in the next stage. Your child does, however, have an interest in others, especially peers, and is beginning to figure out for herself how to be with them. Your child doesn't really have time to mess around with parents much. She acts on an innate urge within herself: her control over her independence.

Because your child trusts you, she tends to challenge you more than anyone. You are safe—yes, believe it or not, you get the pressure because of everything you did right.

Feel relieved. You not only didn't do anything wrong, you are a great asset to your child. She needs a safe workshop in which to practice. You provide that safety.

Your job is to think more broadly with regard to your child than you did before. Expand your limits, while still watching for unsafe environments. Just as you determined how to expand your child's limits when she entered stage three, you'll do it again now.

You really don't have to worry much about your child trying things she is not capable of doing. Your child's cognitive judgment and perceptual skills have increased enough so that she knows how high she can jump or climb. Basically, if your child gets into trouble, it won't be due to a lack of skills.

Your child's inexperience doesn't allow her to know about all the dangers in her environment. She feels invincible. According to the world with which she is familiar, she is invincible. Your job is to protect your child, instilling both caution and powerfulness, without making her feel helpless or overly fearful.

Stubborn, assertive, challenging, and demanding, are apt descriptions of your child during this period. These qualities are geared to help your child develop her sense of powerfulness to meet her own needs.

## What to Do

**Give your child power.**
You have the power to give your child power. If you don't turn power over to your child readily, she'll become increasingly demanding, because the innate drive to care for herself is very strong. Or your child may sneak power behind your back. You don't want this to occur because then you cannot control or guide your child's development of power.

**Teach your child how to take power in acceptable ways.**
The *taking* of power is not so much the problem as *how* your child takes power. Your child needs you to teach her how to take power in ways that are acceptable to you and that fit into society's expectations. You may, for example, say, "It's okay with me if you announce your plans instead of asking me, but I want you to soften your voice when you tell me what you want to do. I don't like to be barked at. That makes me want to tell you, 'No.' A soft voice makes me want to let you do what you wish."

In this way, you teach your child how to be a socially capable, powerful person.

**Affirm your control while respecting your child's need for power.**
Although you give power to your child, you still have to maintain a level of executive control as a parent. You can do this without taking away your child's power. Say, "I'm glad you're telling me what you want to do by using a regular voice. I do have to know about your plans and will be able to agree with them most of the time. But, once in a while, I may have to say 'No.' When I do, I want you to accept what I say. I'll only say 'No' if there is a very good reason."

**Reinforce your child's sense of powerfulness.**
When your child says, "I'm bigger, stronger, or more powerful than you," say, "You bet you are." Speak firmly. Then as an aside say, "At least, most of the time." Then give your child a playful wink. By doing this, you let your child know that you honor her powerfulness, while at the same time you are a solid, protective, powerful support for her; someone who will take the ultimate responsibility for seeing that her needs get met. This will make her feel safe.

You have to continue this approach until your child becomes a young adult. Then it will be time to turn the responsibility for personal power over to your child. For now, your child still needs you behind her. Remember, she's building power. She doesn't yet have it.

## What Not to Do

**Do not prove you are more powerful than your child.**
When your child challenges you, you can, by using fear and brute power, force your child into submission. Doing so robs your child of the ability to develop responsibility and self-control later, and also plants the seeds for rage to develop in your child.

You also rob yourself of the opportunity to have a relationship with a person who loves you and who will turn into a fine, upstanding adult whom you will be pleased to know. Your child's loyalty is yours, if you don't rob her of her power now.

**Do not convey fearfulness in relation to your child's increased independence.**
As your child reaches higher and farther, going ten feet higher in a tree or ten houses farther on the block, you may feel anxiety for her safety. Work with your fears. You may find that by accompanying your child on a walk to friend's house, you are reassured that she knows what she is doing. Or go into the backyard and watch how sure-footed your child is as she climbs the tree. You will become aware that her skills have, in fact, increased, and that your child is much more capable than she was just a short time ago.

**Do not think your child no longer needs you.**
Although you may find it hard to believe that your child needs you, she does. Your child can only be powerful as long as you are there to protect her. Your child needs you, and will for years to come, to be a firm foundation of supportive power—not hurtful power. When you set a limit, explain to your child why she can't do something, and affirm her own powerfulness. In this way, you let your child know that you see what is going on, that you realize what she needs, and that you will not let her power get out of control. This makes your child feel secure.

**Do not hurt your child with your power.**
You can guide your child without hurting her, either physically or emotionally. Using physical force or emotional guilt to make your child do what you want robs her of her budding powerfulness. Show your child what you want and ask her to comply.

Let's say your child wants to cross a busy street by herself so she can visit a new friend. You don't have time to go with her, so you have to tell her no. If you tell your child why she can't cross on her own, but she refuses to listen to you and starts off by herself, simply say, "In this matter, you have no choice. You are not wrong to want to cross the street, but I must pull rank and insist you not go until I can take you. If you continue to try, then I'll have to insist that you stay in the house."

# Building Power

## Your Child's Behavior

In addition to speaking his mind and wanting to be in charge of every aspect of his life, your child may become more physically aggressive at age four.

For example, though your child may have taken peaceful baths up until this time, he may now start a water fight with his brother that ends up with water all over the bathroom floor. He may "steal" cookies from the cookie jar when he knows he's not supposed to, or smear toothpaste all over the bathroom mirror, or start nightly pillow fights with his brother or sister.

You may even get a phone call from the preschool asking you to come in to discuss your child's aggressive behavior.

## What Your Child May Be Thinking or Feeling

What's all the fuss about? I feel powerful! I know how to take charge of what I need. How long will it take for these grownups to realize that I know what I need?

If I want a cookie, I get a cookie. I shouldn't have to ask someone for permission, because I'm big enough to reach the cookie jar. I can do it myself. I'm also strong enough to squeeze the toothpaste tube real hard and make great piles of wormy goo all around the bathroom sink. Last year, I wasn't strong enough to do that.

Mommy is still nice, but she gets in my way a lot these days. So do the other kids at school. Sometimes we all want to be in charge at the same time, and that means I have to fight. I'm pretty strong. I usually win.

Lots of times, I can get my brother to play with me. He'll do almost anything I want him to do. He loves to splash water like me, and we like to hit each other with pillows. We have a great time. But Mommy doesn't seem very happy about it. Sometimes she yells, or just goes into her room.

In school, my teacher has to listen better to what I want to do. I don't want to stand in line when she wants me to or lie down at quiet time anymore. I want to do what I feel is best for me.

## What It Means

First your child discovered his power, then he began to take it, and now he's building it. Turning four means more than growing taller and physically stronger. Your child is also growing emotionally stronger. He needs to prove it to himself. He does that by proving it to you. Your child is just practicing with you.

So everything your child does will be bigger, bolder, and more exaggerated than at any other time in his life. That's only because the skill is new and your child doesn't know how to modulate its expression yet, so he overdoes everything. If a little power is good, a lot seems better.

Your child is not trying to be a hellion. He simply doesn't know how to regulate the amount of power he needs in a situation. Besides, at this age, your child is more familiar with his physical skills than with his emotional and social skills. So your child tends to demonstrate his power physically, rather than simply saying, "Excuse me, but I can't possibly do that."

Your child really believes he can do things that you believe he can't accomplish. After all, your child is overcoming fears and inadequacies from his past, so he has to prove over and over that he can accomplish his new goals. This is the first time your child has actually had goals. Remember how the three-year-old didn't care about goals? Well, the four-year-old definitely cares.

One of your child's goals may be to prove that he is no longer afraid of the dark. Another may be to show how hard he can squeeze a tube of toothpaste. A third may be to see how much noise he can make while getting his older brother to follow his leadership. Your child's intent is not to hurt others. His intent is to prove he can accomplish what he sets out to do.

As a parent, you may feel your child takes risks. Your child doesn't see it that way. Realistically, you will be right some of the time, and he will be right the rest of the time. The skill level of four-year-old children is much higher than at any previous time. Be aware of your child's new skills so you know when to interfere and when to give him room.

Take a deep breath; get support from others, including your child's teacher, who, by the way, can use your support in return; set some new firm limits; and introduce a large element of laughter into your child-rearing practices.

## What to Do

**Gather your own support system around you.**
At this stage, one of your best resources is a group of adults who likes children and understands what you face. The group can consist of teachers, other parents, family members, and anyone interested in child development. From this array of people you can learn what's "normal," while gaining support; there is power in numbers.

It's not us against them, but you will benefit from healthy, positive support at this time. You can share ideas on handling four-year-olds. You can laugh at some of your child's antics (not at your child), and you can feel reinforced when you need to maintain a firm limit.

**Be clear about a few limits.**
You've already decided to support your child's powerfulness and contain it within firm limits. Now your job is to sort out the most important limits for the moment. You may decide that your child may not be destructive toward people or things. You may decide that your child may not go out alone at night because it is simply too dangerous. And you may decide that your child may not be disruptive at preschool.

On the other hand, you may decide that having a pillow fight with his brother once each night is really not so bad after all, especially if the kids put the pillows back on the bed afterwards. Or you may choose to overlook a few missing cookies or respond to the pile of toothpaste only with, "Next time, please find something less expensive to squeeze out of a tube."

**Have direct, growth-producing repercussions to broken limits.**
Once you decide which limits belong in a "must do" category, you must follow through firmly, not angrily or punitively, with repercussions that teach your child and make the situation better. When your child acts aggressively toward another child, stop the play and remind your child to use words to explain what he wants, just like you did when he was two and three. However, this time, add, "I

cannot let you play with Jimmy unless you treat him right. You can't always get what you want when you want it. Sometimes you can be boss, but sometimes Jimmy needs to be boss."

Then have your child take a time-out for a few minutes. Five or ten minutes is long enough for this age; any longer proves ineffective for teaching the lesson. The time-out tells your child that he must treat the other child properly; if he doesn't, he may not play with the other child.

**Work with other adults to help your child control his power.**
In group settings, such as preschool and neighborhood playgroups, you must work with other adults to define expectations for your child. Other adults may have different expectations for your child. Clarify these, and agree on some general guidelines.

If an adult has very different expectations, due to different values or child-rearing methods, you may have to move your child out of the group. For example, if a preschool teacher believes children should jump the moment they are told to jump, and you want to teach your child to think for himself, you probably have to change the setting in which you place your child.

**Occasionally let your children gang up on you.**
Reversing the normal flow of power in the family can buy you cooperation. Let your children gang up on you in fairly benign situations. Allow them to stay up an hour later than usual on a weekend night; this is a good way to let your children feel their powerfulness. Your children do, however, have to express their power in acceptable terms. No temper tantrums, whining, or nagging allowed.

## What Not to Do

**Do not let your child's behavior make you dislike him.**
After you establish the limits that you believe are truly important for your child, maintain those limits so your child doesn't become unlikable to you. Sure, what your child does may displease you, but that doesn't mean you have to dislike your child. However, if you let your child "get away" with unlikable behavior much of the time,

you may begin to dislike your child.

An occasional feeling of dislike is normal. However, a child out of control is very taxing. Get outside help in the form of counseling if you are unable to get control of the situation yourself. You have not necessarily done anything wrong, and you most certainly have nothing of which to be ashamed. Neither is your child bad. No counselor will blame you. Instead, you can receive help to make your home a happy place to raise your child and to live in moderate peace.

**Do not use brute force to limit your child's power.**
Physical punishment and force may temporarily appear to limit your child's expressions of power, but in the long run, the price tag proves enormous. Either your child loses his valuable emotional powerfulness, so that later he is unable to become a responsible person, or he becomes rageful and later takes his rage out on others who are less strong than he. Your child becomes a perpetrator.

To limit your child's power, you must use nonviolent, nonforceful, firm techniques. If your child does something of which you don't approve, use words to communicate sensible consequences. For example, if your child damages property, you can say calmly but firmly, "When you do that, you will have to pay to fix the property. You may not hurt things. Let's see how much it costs and what you have to do to make it right." If your child hits another child, hitting your child only reinforces the very thing you don't want him to do. Instead, say, "You may not play with your friend until you are able to control yourself. You may not hit another person. You can use your words to say what you do and don't like. You must spend time in your room now, to get back your control."

**Do not allow your child to stay out of control.**
Be sure that your child is ready for the learning situation in which you place him. Some children become easily overstimulated in large groups. Others, who have been subjected to some form of abuse, may "act out" their hurt and damage on other children or adults. Occasionally, a child has an organic or physical condition that makes it harder than usual for him to control his behavior. Yet, at four, these children will be building power just like other four-

year-olds. Without the ability to curb their expressions of power, these children may need extra help.

If any of these situations apply to your child, you must evaluate the problem and arrange for whatever help you and your child need. Other people don't have to put up with your child's behavior. Your child's aggressiveness is a symptom that something is amiss. Neither you nor your child is bad, but a problem exists and it must be remedied.

Most children who are aggressive at this age, however, simply express their power incorrectly. Most will outgrow this stage. One day your child may act very nicely, as he did when he was three, and the next, your child may act responsibly, as a five-year-old. Your child's changing behavior helps you know that your child is progressing normally.

# Testing Power

## Your Child's Behavior

You may notice that your child plays one parent off of the other at this age. For example, if you tell your daughter she can't have any candy before dinner, she may sulk and cry. But when she's alone with your spouse, she may try to talk that parent into letting her have the candy. Not knowing that the child has already been told no, the parent may say okay.

In fact, just when you start to understand or get used to your child being bossy, argumentative, and even aggressive, your child may start this new behavior to get what she wants. Who wins when this happens? Often, you feel as though your daughter does.

## What Your Child May Be Thinking or Feeling

If I really want a piece of candy and Mommy says I can't have it, I feel frustrated. I get angry because I feel so helpless. Mommy and Daddy said they are tired of my arguments and fights, so I'll have to figure out a new way to get that candy. Daddy didn't say I couldn't have the candy, so maybe I'll ask him. If he gives it to me, I bet Mommy won't take it away. I know she won't take Daddy's candy away from him or tell him no.

See how smart I am to figure things out? I figured out a way to get the piece of candy I need, and I didn't fight or scream or yell. This way, I can get what I want and not make too much noise or get into trouble.

## What It Means

In the last two stages of development, your child's chief concern was her relationship to the objects in her environment. Now her interest shifts from things to people and what they can do for her. Your child doesn't yet have true empathy. That won't come until age five or so.

Your child uses people at this stage, not because she's mean, hard-hearted, or a psychopath. She just hasn't yet developed beyond seeing people as objects. This is natural. You haven't done anything wrong.

During the third stage of your child's development, she already learned that she can manipulate objects. Now your child wants to try her hand at manipulating people. She is uncannily good at it. After all, your child watches the people around her and models herself on them.

Your child also prefers to stay out of trouble, though that may be hard for you to believe due to the large amount of it she finds at this age. Your child prefers to have you on her side rather than in opposition. Only when your child has to choose between getting something she wants and getting your approval does she cast you aside. As your child matures through the fourth stage, she'll discover more and more ways to get both.

Playing one parent against the other is a variation on manipulation. With innocent things, such as a piece of candy shared with a newly arrived parent, you may as well smile. In a way, your smile tells your child that you see what she did—you are no fool, after all—but that you will give her this one.

When, however, the manipulation involves one of the more serious limits you have set, you must stop the behavior. The best way to stop the unwanted behavior is for the parents to get together, agree on the limits, and present a solid front. The trouble comes when the parents don't and can't agree. Then the child, in a sense, is forced to play one against the other, and she loses in the long run.

Manipulation has gotten a bad reputation, but it doesn't necessarily mean that it is bad. Everyone does it all the time. Let's suppose you want the cashier at the grocery store to work a little faster and speak to you in a friendly tone. All you have to do is smile, ask how his or her day is going, and show empathy. Try it. The cashier will speed up. That's manipulation.

Suppose you want your spouse to feel good about your night out with your friends. You suggest that you go out to dinner the day before, and you say that you've been thinking that it would be good for your spouse to have a night out with friends, and that you'd be glad to cover with the kids. Thinking of your spouse's preferences and needs is a good way to manipulate your spouse into feeling good about watching the kids while you are out having a good time. This is how your child learns.

## What to Do

**Know what's really important.**
Recall which guidelines and limits are truly important and remember to let your child win in other areas. Smile, or even say, "Honey, you sure pulled one over on me this time." By acknowledging your observation of her win, you support your child's budding growth of powerfulness and you let her know that you know what's going on.

**Teach your child how to manipulate you in acceptable ways.**
Go right ahead and honestly say, "My job is to teach you how to get what you need from me. When you talk in a regular voice, smile, and help me out rather than make messes, I want to help you get what you want. When you argue with me about things, it makes me not want to help you." Your four-year-old can read those messages loud and clear.

Don't compromise the important issues, though it is wise to consider ways to negotiate something that is really important to each of you. For example, if you don't want your child to eat cookies before bedtime without brushing her teeth afterward because she has had some dental problems, say, "Honey, I have to insist: don't sneak a cookie before going to bed. I'd rather have you pick and save one for your lunch tomorrow. If, however, you have to have a cookie before you go to bed, tell me. We'll find a small one and we'll brush your teeth a second time." Then ask, "Will that work for you? It'll work for me."

By negotiating and asking your child how she feels, you will probably win your child over. She likes being treated with respect, so she goes along with your suggestions. And because you taught your child how to reach a mutually acceptable compromise, she is more likely to cooperate with you next time.

**Let your child test your limits within your boundaries.**
Testing your limits doesn't mean abandoning your limits. Rather, let your child know which limits are mandatory and which limits are flexible. Teach your child the difference.

You may find it helpful to try three different types of limits:

1. Nonnegotiable limits, such as, "You may not hit or hurt another person or thing";

2. Negotiable limits, such as, "We'll talk about some way for both of us to get what we want";

3. Released limits, such as "You decide what outfit you want to wear." A released limit turns the power totally over to your four-year-old.

## What Not to Do

**Don't have one set of limits one day and a different set the next.**
Be consistent with the limits you set. Don't vacillate on them, depending on your mood and schedule. If you decide to change a limit, do it openly and honestly. Let your child know about the change and explain the reason for it. Don't change a lot of limits a lot of the time.

**Do not scold your child for manipulating.**
Show your child how to manipulate according to your terms. She is only doing what is humanly natural. Your child is not doing something wrong; she is only doing something you don't like.

**Do not confuse your child's powerfulness with your dissatisfaction.**
When your child acts powerfully and manipulates you, you may not get what you want, especially if what you want is a child who behaves the way you want. By squelching your child's power to get what you want, you deny your child the opportunity to become a responsible person. Instead, show your child how she can give you what you want and retain her power.

# Pushing Your Limits

## Your Child's Behavior

Four-year-olds lie and even take things that don't belong to them. That is not unusual—even if they've been taught, since they were babies, that lying and stealing are wrong.

In fact, at this age, your child may take something from a store and then lie about it when you confront him. If you ask your child why he took the item without asking you to pay for it, he may answer, "I found it," or "I don't know." And if you tell you child to put his shoes back on so you can go to the store to return the item, he may refuse.

## What Your Child May Be Thinking or Feeling

I forgot that I put that packet of gum in my pocket at the store. I meant to chew it all up really fast. But now Mommy's found it. From the sound of her voice, I think I'm in big trouble. I feel really scared inside. I feel so scared that I think I'd better hide what I did. I'm not sure why I took the gum. Maybe I'll say that I found it in the street.

I know I'm not supposed to take what belongs to other people, but I wasn't sure about taking things from the store. Mommy and Daddy pick up lots of things at the store. The things in the store don't seem to belong to anyone in particular. I know that Mommy and Daddy pay someone for the things they pick up before they leave the store, but since I didn't have any money, I just thought I'd skip that last step. I really wanted some gum. I didn't think it would matter to the store. They had a lot of gum. I knew they wouldn't miss one little pack.

When Mommy sounds so mad at me, I get scared and I have to puff myself up twice as big to really let her know that I'm strong and powerful. That way, I know that I'm strong and powerful, too.

Now she says I have to put my shoes on so we can take the gum back to the store. Maybe if I show her who's boss, I won't feel so scared. I'm afraid to go back to the store. I don't know what the store person will do to me. I don't know what Mommy will do to me. If I don't put my shoes on, I won't have to go to the store. So I won't put my shoes on.

## What It Means

As your child progresses through age four, he not only gains more independence than he's ever had before, but he tries to figure out where all the limits are. Your child can now do so much more than he could before that you may have to extend the old limits in some cases and reduce them in others.

In the past, your child used to only be able to go two houses on either side of yours; now he can go eight or ten. Your child used to have to hold your hand in the store; now he can go get things off the shelves. Your child even knows how to pay the cashier and wait for the change.

Your child's leadership skills are emerging, and sometimes he even acts nicely to other children as he directs them in a project. Little signs of maturity are emerging; what a relief. Before, you worried that all the power building your child was doing may not translate into good behavior. Now you feel joyful that he is turning into the well-behaved child you dreamed of raising.

Because you've been doing things right, your child feels safe enough to test yet another limit. Every time your child succeeds at mastering a limit, he reaches a new plateau. The next step makes him ready to reach further and experiment even more.

Sure, your child knows he's to leave other people's things alone, but who owns the gum in the store? He's not yet clear about that. Going through the ritual of paying for gum at a checkout counter, especially when your child really doesn't yet have the capability to figure out the math, is a mechanical process to your child. He doesn't fully understand what he is doing.

Returning the gum to the store and having your child pay for it won't teach him about the abstract concept of buying and selling, but it will teach him the process he must go through to take gum out of the store.

At four, your child is not a thief. He didn't even really steal, though it looks that way from an adult perspective. Rather, your child is trying to figure out how the world works.

As your child progresses through the year, he may begin to test some of your limits by again taking something from a store or by bringing a toy home from his friend's house or from preschool. Your child is testing whether you will follow through the same way you did the first time.

When your child takes things, how you respond is important. Your job is to teach your child the rules and repercussions of taking what doesn't belong to him. Many children also test limits about taking things at age six and even eight. After that, a child who takes things is giving a cry for help; he is displaying a symptom. But that is not the case at age four.

When your child lies to you, he's afraid to tell the truth. Although your child may not exactly know what he's done wrong, he senses he's done something that will displease you. Your four-year-old, despite the way he acts, does still want your approval. Your job is to make it safe to tell the truth.

As your child learns these large life lessons, he will have to add to his own feelings of powerfulness. Your child does this by appearing defiant and by disobeying you. He's trying to trick himself into believing he's powerful. In reality, your child feels less than mighty inside. Your job is to keep as cool a head as possible, teach your child how to get what he needs, and know he's acting quite normal for his age.

## What to Do

**Help your child return anything he's taken that's not his.**
When your child comes home with an item that he didn't pay for or that wasn't given to him, go with him and show him how to return the item and make what he did right. Say, "I'll go with you to take the gum back." Then tell your child what to do. Say, "Give it to the clerk and hand him the money to pay for it."

Even if half of the gum is chewed, take the package back and have your child pay for it. If your child doesn't have any money, give him a job at home to earn the money to pay for the gum. Do this as soon after your discovery as you can, so the effect is not lost.

At four, your child must be taught how to make his error right. The first time he takes something that is not his, you don't have to make him apologize, because he didn't intend to do anything wrong. Later, if your child again takes something that doesn't belong to him, instead of apologizing, your child will learn more if you have him say, "I'm learning to take only what belongs to me. Here's the money to pay for the gum so it belongs to me."

**Make your child feel safe to be honest with you.**
When your child lies to you, say, "The most important thing in the world is for you to be honest with me. I must be able to trust you. When you tell me the truth, I can help you fix anything that's wrong, and that will be the end of it. If you tell me a lie, then you not only have to fix the problem, but I'll have to see that you lose privileges because you lied."

Make it worthwhile for your child to tell you the truth. Of course, if you want your child to be truthful, you also must model truthfulness.

**Be firm with your limits, teaching your child what you want of him.**
Your job is to continue to be your child's teacher. Punishment has no place in this process because it doesn't teach anything. You do, however, have to apply repercussions for your child's behavior if he continues to do what you've taught him not to do.

Be sure, though, that your teaching is clear. Sometimes adults assume a child understands something when really he doesn't. For example, a child may know not to take what belongs to another person, but in his mind, a store is not another person.

**Tell your child what you do and don't like about his behavior.**
When your child acts defiant, doesn't mind you, or does something you don't like, say, "I don't like it when you refuse to put your shoes on to go to the store to return the gum."

Differentiate between your love and care for your child and your approval of his behavior. Say, "I love you and care about you enough to teach you how to be an honest person, so people can like you and trust you. I don't like it when you refuse to cooperate with me."

**Be honest with your child.**
When your child acts defiantly, you must be honest in return. Say,

"I can't force you to put your shoes on, but I am asking you. I won't hit you or hurt you to make you do it, but when you don't cooperate with me, it makes me not want to help you." Then let the issue go and, if necessary, go to the store with a shoeless four-year-old. When your child wants something a little later, say, "I don't feel like cooperating because you wouldn't cooperate with me earlier when I wanted you to wear your shoes." Say this in a matter-of-fact voice, not punitively, harshly, or in a tone that conveys, "So now I'll fix you."

**Be sure you are a model of truthfulness and honesty.**
The most powerful teaching tool for truthfulness and honesty is you. Live the way you want your child to live.

## What Not to Do

**Do not think of your child as a liar or a thief.**
Realize that your child's behavior is innocent at this stage and that he doesn't yet fully understand what is needed from him. If you label your child a liar or a thief, you actually plant that idea in his head, and he begins to see himself in that way. Such labeling tends to bring about the outcome you most fear.

**Do not let your child fail to return what doesn't belong to him.**
Your child must immediately return anything that he has taken that doesn't belong to him. That is the only way your child will learn what is expected of him. Talking about it won't work. Sure, you may be dog tired, it's late and raining out, and the store closes in five minutes so you may not get there in time, but try. The sooner the return is made after the item is taken, the more effective the learning process. Consider the long-term ramifications. Don't blow off one little package of gum.

**Do not punish your child for lying.**
Some parents use brutal tactics, such as washing the child's mouth out with soap, spanking, and more, to try to teach their child to tell the truth. These methods only discharge the fear felt by the parent. They miss the point with the child. Make it safe for your child to

tell the truth.

Of course, the child must be responsible for fixing or helping to fix whatever results from his behavior. But rather than punishing your child for going beyond a limit, compliment your child for telling the truth. For example, suppose your child plays ball in the house when you specifically asked him not to, and while playing, he accidentally breaks a vase. If, when you ask how the vase broke, your child says, "I broke it while I was playing ball," you should say, "I'm really glad you told me the truth about how the vase got broken. I appreciate your truthfulness." You may then give your child a hug before continuing, "You'll have to earn some money to pay for a new vase, and I will remind you again not to play ball in the house. Now you know why I don't want you to—because you can break things. I know you will remember. Because you were truthful, you will not be punished, but you must fix what was hurt."

This way, your child learns that he can safely tell you the truth, and he learns to be responsible for his actions.

# Exploring

## Your Child's Behavior

Your four-year-old probably goes strong all day long, from one activity to the next. One minute she's outside digging for worms in the dirt, and the next minute she's climbing the tree in the backyard. One minute she's one person's best friend, and the next minute, she wants to go to someone else's house. One minute she's playing quietly, and the next minute she's crying because she fell off a fence she was trying to climb.

Along with all this busyness, your child may have some toileting accidents. Even if she has been "potty trained" since age two, she may start to have accidents, even several times a week. Although you may be concerned about this, your child may not.

If you ask your child why she has these accidents, she may tell you, "I'm busy."

## What Your Child May Be Thinking or Feeling

Right when I'm having a good time, I have to go to the bathroom. But I don't want to stop what I'm doing. I'll just finish this first. Whoops! I wet my pants. I don't think the older kids I play with have this kind of problem. I wonder why they don't wet their pants when they are outside playing away from home for so long.

I'm sure glad Mommy doesn't get upset with me. She lets me put my clothes in the washing machine. I can even start it now, if there are other things to wash.

Earlier this week, I had to stop playing because I fell off the fence and hit my head and Mommy had to take me to the doctor. I like my doctor. She talks really nice to me and lets me use her stethoscope. She made Mommy smile when she said my head was okay.

I don't think Mommy should worry about me climbing the fence. I was just trying to reach the top to see how far down the street I could see from there. I wondered if I could see all the way to my friend's house.

Usually when I try to climb something, I don't fall. But a bee flew at me, and when I tried to shoo it away, I slipped. I can do almost anything I want to do these days. If I need the jar of jelly from the top of the kitchen shelf, all I have to do is climb up on the counter, open the cupboard door, and jump up to the top shelf. I only fell one time when I tried that, and I don't think it was my fault that I broke a lot of Mommy's dishes when I fell.

## What It Means

Part of being four means your child is once again expanding her range of activity. She's ready and fairly able to take on a lot more of the world. To do this, she begins exploring, not just territory, but all the things she wants to do.

Because this whole stage is about your child acquiring power, your child will rarely ask you whether she can do something new. You're lucky if she tells you what she's about to do. Mostly she'll just do it.

Problems arise because your child still doesn't know a whole lot about the world. She doesn't know that cupboard doors don't stay where you put them. They swing back and forth and even pinch fingers and knock feet off shelves. She doesn't know that kitchen shelves are not for climbing—at least, she doesn't know these things until she tries them out for herself.

So you see, it's not that she is more clumsy. Rather, your child is trying to do a whole lot more than before, and she's discovering the limits to her skills. Actually, your child is probably amazingly adept at managing the things she's trying to do. She'll soon learn a whole new set of nature's limits.

From an adult perspective, you may think your child should ask how things work or how to accomplish whatever task she's after. But from a four-year-old perspective, that would feel like giving away some of her newfound power. Besides, your child figures that you may tell her she can't do whatever it is she wants to do. She's not taking that chance.

Often your child gets caught up in activities with her friends. As she enjoys playing with other children, your child discovers that sometimes they follow her lead and sometimes she follows someone else's. Many heads definitely come up with a lot more things to get into. But remember, the intent is innocent. The kids are just exploring.

As busy as your child is these days, you can understand that she doesn't have time for mundane things, such as taking the time to go to the bathroom. She's not having toileting accidents the way she did at two. Probably nothing at all is wrong with her bladder. Instead, your child puts off going to the bathroom. She puts it off so long that even if she starts home, she can't make it in time.

Don't worry. Your child will get her timing down better. It just takes a little while to work toileting, eating, and managing other daily chores into her busy play schedule.

## What to Do

**Handle your child's toileting accidents calmly.**
If your child goes through a period of toileting accidents, talk with her about the importance of taking a break. Explain that adults take breaks at home and at work. You may pick out a hero or heroine of your child's and explain how that person handles daily living activities. Even astronauts, sports heroes, and Batman have to go to the bathroom.

Remind your child to take a break as she goes off to play. If that is not enough to encourage her to take a break, and if you're getting tired of the soiled clothes, tell your child you'll call her midmorning to remind her. If your child challenges you, add, "If you don't come when I call, you won't be able to play outside this afternoon." But don't start with the limits at first. Usually, toileting accidents can be handled without pressure.

**Explain to your child how and why accidents happen.**
After you've comforted your injured child and tended to any wounds, physical or emotional, talk about what happened. DON'T SCOLD. Teach your child how to avoid an accident the next time.

**Reassure your child that she is doing a good job taking care of herself.**
Your child is aware of the accidents and inadequacies she experiences. Most likely, she covers her fears and uncertainties with bravado. "I don't need anyone," is the reaction you're likely to hear. But your child does need you and your support. Afraid that she will be criticized—even if you've tried very hard to be nonjudgmental—

your child is likely to hide her needs from you. Your job is to offer support, even when unasked. Make your statements simple. Drop them in an incidental way rather than having a serious talk with your child. You can say, "You sure have become a capable person. You know a lot about how to handle things." You may want to be specific by saying, "You sure climbed that wall great." Sometimes act surprised, saying, "I didn't know you were that strong."

**Differentiate really dangerous situations from others.**
If you try to limit everything your child wants to try, she will tune you out completely. If, however, you acknowledge your child's capability in some areas and label other feats as "Really Dangerous," your child will tend to listen to you. Be sure to show your child what is so really dangerous about the actions you've identified, and explain why you want her to avoid them.

## What Not to Do

**Do not scold your child after an accident.**
Scolding turns off your child's hearing. Your child will not learn from the accident. Instead, become a teacher and explain why the accident happened. You may want to brush up on your physics, because a lot of accidents during this time have to do with your child's physical activity. Simplify your explanation, but do teach your child how things work.

**Do not call your four-year-old a baby.**
Although your child may have toileting accidents, as she did when she was a baby, the reasons are different. Calling your child a baby, even if it works to stop the accidents, damages your child psychologically. Years from now your child will have trouble anytime she feels helpless—like a baby. Instead, reassure your four-year-old that she will regain control over her body very soon. Tell your child that the toileting accident is a normal reaction to the busy schedule she keeps. Then help your child remember to care for her physical needs.

**Do not become overprotective during this period.**
Since your child's likelihood of accidents is increased, a tendency to be protective makes sense to you. However, be careful not to

overprotect your child. Your child can learn to be cautious without becoming fearful. That is her job for the moment. Teach your child. Show her how things work. Encourage your child to let you know when she needs something, and then be sure you let her follow through; don't do the job for her. The reward will be a self-assured, skillful, powerful-feeling child.

# Protecting Himself

## Your Child's Behavior

You may find your four-year-old using language you know he hasn't heard at home to bully other children. For example, your child may act aggressively and menacingly toward a child who tries to cross your yard. If your child plays with a younger child, your child may order the younger child around more than he actually plays with him on an equal footing.

If you try to talk about this kind of behavior with your child, he may explain to you that he's trying to show everyone that he knows how to be the boss.

You may not like the way your child treats some of the other children, but you may also notice that your child is becoming quite a leader. You may wonder whether you should be angry at him, or encourage him to develop this leadership potential.

## What Your Child May Be Thinking or Feeling

Boy, do I feel big and tough these days. Just look at everything I can do! I know where my neighbor's yard ends and mine begins. I know how to climb trees and fences.

In fact, I'm so big and strong that I'll show the little kid next door who's boss. He's only three, but I'm four. I heard an older kid call another kid "dummy," so I think I'll use that word on this little kid.

Wow, he sure reacted to that. He stopped right in his tracks. I guess "dummy" is a good word to use when you're showing someone who's boss. It might be fun to play with him, even though he's a baby, because no one else is around. I'll pretend I'm in charge and that I know exactly what I'm doing.

Now I see that Mommy's watching us. I know I'll really impress her. I'd like to play with this kid's truck. I'll act tough to be sure I get to play with it. Look how he does whatever I tell him to do. I guess I'm even stronger and tougher than I thought!

I like the way it feels to have someone do exactly what I tell them to do. At home, I'm always supposed to do what Mommy and Daddy tell me to do. Sometimes I'd like to tell them what to do.

## What It Means

Your child has to develop his powerfulness. The urge to be in charge of what he does comes innately. You will notice that your child acts powerfully, but his power is often exerted over someone else, rather than emerging as a true feeling from inside. Your child hasn't yet learned how to be firm instead of forceful.

Calling names, scaring others, and making demands are all ways that your child protects himself. Inside he feels vulnerable. Mommy and Daddy and other adults protected him up until now. He's taking over the job of protecting himself now, and he's not very confident. So your child acts extra tough to convince others that he has power. Really he's trying to prove to himself that he is big and strong. In addition, your child's feelings of powerfulness are easily squelched by fear that he won't be able to get what he needs on his own.

Previously, your child learned to manipulate toys and objects. Now he's practicing manipulating people. Younger children often serve as objects of his manipulation.

Since manipulation allows a person to be in control, it, too, serves as protection—a way for your child to get what he thinks or feels he needs. Often the term manipulation is used in a derogatory sense. However, don't forget that someone who manipulates another person uses the only way he knows to get something. Teach the person a better way to get his needs met, and he'll use it.

So, too, with four-year-olds. Teach them to be aware of what they need and to honestly communicate those needs, and they will not have to manipulate you. Or teach your child to manipulate in acceptable terms, that is, in ways in which you approve. Then you have taught your child a useful skill.

When you let your child make choices at this age, your child feels more assured that he'll get what he needs than when someone simply tells him what to do. Choices provide feelings of powerfulness. Along with the ability to say no, teach your child to set limits on others, which is another form of protection. Let your child know it's okay to ask someone to leave if that person is messing with his things. Or show your child with your actions how to nicely set limits on others. Your child will hear you tell the woman on the phone no when you say, "I wish I could help you, but I can't take the time now to bake five dozen cookies. Ask me next month if you'd like."

Sure, your child wants attention now. But that, too, means he's learning to guide others' awareness toward himself. When your child can do this, he can manipulate or steer that person in the direction he needs or wants. By gaining attention, your child is in the driver's seat. And remember, all the skills your child builds now will allow him to lead and guide others later in life.

## What to Do

**Teach your child about the need to be self-protective.**
Every child should be taught to protect himself. Explain how sometimes everyone, even grownups, feel weak or vulnerable when they are around someone stronger than they are. Be sure to say that nothing is wrong with that feeling.

Next, explain how we have to find ways to protect ourselves—but that these ways should help us without hurting others. You may say, "When someone tells you to do something you don't want to do, you could kick them, but then you'd get in trouble with me. Instead, you can use your words to say, 'No, I don't want to,' or 'My mommy won't let me.' Then you won't get in trouble with me. Then come and tell me what happened, right away."

Be sure to tell your child to use you as an excuse anytime he feels threatened by someone. And tell him to tell you immediately about what happened.

**Set firm limits on any hurtful behavior toward others.**
Stop your child when he calls other children names or takes advantage of younger or less-able children. Although you want your child to get what he needs to develop his sense of powerfulness, he may not, under any conditions, do so by taking advantage of others.

Instead, teach your child alternative ways to get what he needs. You could say, "Tell the other child that you like his truck and then ask whether you can borrow it for a while." Show him how to do this.

**Teach your child how to manipulate you.**
You will find yourself ahead of the game if you tell your child at an early stage how you want him to treat you to get what he wants. Say, "If you want me to take you somewhere, ask me in a normal

voice and I'll try my best. If you nag or whine or cry, I definitely will not take you."

**Support your child's attempts at self-protection.**
When your child tries to protect himself, give your approval by saying, "I'm glad to see that you are protecting yourself." Then add, if you feel it is necessary, "I do, however, need you to speak in a nice tone of voice." Or you may say, "Under no circumstances may you call someone a dummy, but you may tell the person that you'd rather he didn't come in your yard right now."

## What Not to Do

**Do not force your child to do things he doesn't want to do.**
Although some parents think that children should automatically obey them, such an approach only teaches powerlessness, which will surface later as a problem. Children who are not taught to appropriately take their power become either victims or perpetrators in later life. Neither makes a self-responsible person. Both cost the person and our society dearly.

**Do not expect your child to protect himself against big odds.**
Letting your four-year-old stand alone against older children, where he constantly loses, usually has one of two consequences: the child feels that he always has to fight for everything, or the child learns to feel helpless for the rest of his life, as though he can never win. Your child needs your protection so chronic problems don't develop. However, remember to only protect your child to the extent that he can't protect himself. Don't overprotect.

**Do not punish your child for questioning your limits.**
By allowing your child to negotiate with you, you teach your child a valuable skill that he can use in later life. Just be sure that he speaks in a reasonable voice: no whining, nagging, or threatening.

You may want to have two categories of limits: negotiable and nonnegotiable. Negotiable limits can include deciding bedtime, choosing clothing, and using spending money. Nonnegotiable limits may include telling you where he is going, being gentle with others, and telling the truth. Clearly label limits that come up over time, and be consistent with your application of limits.

# Losing Power

## Your Child's Behavior

You may notice that your child tries to be in charge of everything most of the time, but sometimes she just gives up and dissolves into tears. For example, sometimes your child fights to make sure she gets her turn at a game, and other times she just cries if she can't have the first turn. Or your child argues for hours with a friend about a game rule, but she bursts into tears when Daddy wins at arm wrestling (a game she wanted to play).

Your child may seem in control one day and almost helpless the next. Sometimes she wants to play Wonder Woman and show her strength as she tears around the house. And other times, she wants to curl up in your lap and have you rub her back. At those times, your child is more like a little baby than the take-charge general who orders everyone else around the house.

Although you try, you may not really understand your four-year-old child much of the time. You'd like to, though, because you may not like walking around on eggshells, wondering whether you should protect and support your child or take cover as she tears through her day.

## What Your Child May Be Thinking or Feeling

Sometimes I like to yell really loudly and be big and strong and run around to show everyone how much I can do and how much I know. I like to make decisions for myself, and I can sure stand up for myself.

But sometimes I don't have enough power, like when I arm wrestle Daddy, and that makes me scared. He's so big, and I mean really big. When he beats me at arm wrestling, I feel helpless, and that feels very bad. I want to tell him to stop beating me at that game, but I'm afraid if I tell him that, he won't want to play with me anymore. I don't know what to do when I get that feeling. Sometimes I just cry.

When I get tired, I feel powerless. All my power goes away. That is a very bad feeling, but I hate taking naps. They're for little kids, not for big four-year-olds. Sometimes when I'm tired, I like to curl up with Mommy for a while. That way I can get a little rest, but I don't have to admit that I'm tired.

No one seems to really understand me now. Sometimes, I don't really understand myself, either. That makes me feel powerless, too. It's really hard being four.

## What It Means

During the year to year and a half in which your child's main task is to develop her powerfulness, she will experience many ups and downs. Just as adults have problems with feeling powerful under certain conditions, so does your child. We are all more susceptible to powerlessness when we are hungry, angry, lonely, or tired. Children are not much different.

Losing power feels bad. Your child needs extra help from you when her power is threatened. Watch for situations where power loss occurs.

Playing with a parent or older child whom your child knows and loves makes her susceptible to two sets of feelings. On one hand, your child trusts the person, so she lets her defenses down. On the other hand, because your child tends to see the person as a protector and helper, if that person takes her power away, she feels a double loss (as in the arm wrestling incident).

When your child plays with a friend, though, she doesn't have this problem because she doesn't turn to the friend for trusted support, nurturing, and protection. Your child's friend is a peer with whom your child is on equal footing, so she can yell to her heart's content. The yelling, in part, is a game.

Sometimes children and parents get into what is called a power struggle. That's when both parties fight over something where only one person can win. "You will put on your galoshes," says the mother. "No I won't," says the child. Back and forth they yell, sometimes upgrading the level of threats.

Let's suppose it's winter and you are trying to get your four-year-old ready to go to the store. You say, "If you don't put on your galoshes, your friend can't come over to play."

"I don't care. I don't want to wear my galoshes," says your child.

In desperation, you say, "If you don't put on your galoshes now, I won't buy you the new doll I promised you."

"Keep the old doll," she says.

"Don't speak to me that way. Get your galoshes on, right now," you say.

By now you are both probably worn down, distraught, and deep into a hole from which there is no graceful exit. If you win, your child loses power. If she wins, you lose, and she loses because she's lost a protectively powerful mother.

The best way to help your child keep her power while you still get what you need—in this case, warm coverings on your child's feet—is to take the time to discover why she doesn't want to wear galoshes. Then explain about the cold weather and give your child a choice. You may offer, "Would you rather wear your galoshes or your heavy shoes?" Or you may offer an alternative: "Would you be willing to wear your galoshes unbuckled to the car and then take them off inside the car?" Often, children this age like something different and are willing to try any novel way of doing things, such as wearing their galoshes unbuckled.

The whole issue here is to keep your child from losing power during this important power-building stage.

## What to Do

**Determine whether your child is playing power games.**
Such games as tug-of-war, or arguing about whose turn it is, build power in young children. They are not meant for adult intervention. Stay out of the way unless you are getting tired of the noise. Then simply say, "Please lower your voices."

**Give your child an unfair advantage when playing with older people.**
If an adult or older child plays any game with your child, they will always win. At this age, repeated losing causes your child to feel too much loss of power. Let your child win sometimes. You can pretend to let your child beat you at arm wrestling. Don't fear you're turning your child into some kind of weakling. It won't be long until your child can begin to accept losing without losing power.

**Let your child become a "baby" from time to time without losing power.**

If your child doesn't want to take a nap, don't insist, but when you notice she's tired, give your child alternative opportunities to rest. You may have your child lie down for thirty minutes, telling her she doesn't have to sleep but she does need to rest. Or you may sit with her as she cuddles next to you. Of course, she may fall asleep—then again, she may not. In any case, enjoy the cuddling and the quiet time together because, I promise you, these precious times will soon become few and far between. Enjoy them while they last.

## What Not to Do

**Do not let your child be overpowered by anyone.**

Very unfortunately, children of this age are often severely punished for asserting themselves. Sometimes the loss of power happens when an adult shames the child. Other times, adults use guilt to get the upper hand. In all cases, the adult wins at the expense of the child.

The obvious power of an adult over a child proves nothing. Meanwhile, the child loses the opportunity to turn into an emotionally strong person who doesn't have to victimize another.

Often, an adult who overpowers a child was once either the victim of someone's power or watched someone overpower another, less-strong person. In domestic violence situations, the child is keenly affected by watching one parent abuse the other. The child feels helpless to assist the victimized adult and guilty for not being able to do something.

Protect your child from people who are overpowering.

**Do not try to teach your child to lose at this age.**

Your child will be ready to lose sometimes at games and activities during the next stage of development, so wait until your child reaches that stage to teach losing. Prematurely pressing a child to "play fair" and "take it like a grownup" only retards the child's ability to truly acquire these skills.

**Do not force your child to do things.**

The use of force never yields the results you want. To be sure, it may look as though you got what you wanted now, but ultimately you and your child will lose.

Sooner or later, your child will grow big enough to be no longer dependent upon you, and then she will stand up to you, run away, or sabotage herself or you. Many a teen hurts a parent by hurting herself, whether by failing in school, drinking excessively, or having more than the average number of accidents. The seeds for these problems are laid down during your child's fourth year. Let your child have choices and options now, and you will raise a self-reliant, responsible, protective teenager.

# Expressing Power Emotionally

## Your Child's Behavior

You may notice that your child has frequent temper tantrums and seems to be very dramatic about everything at this age. You may start to hear very strong emotional words, such as "hate," when your child describes something or someone he dislikes. If your child feels very frustrated or angry because of something you said to him, he may even use the word "hate" when talking to you.

Although such language can be very hurtful, it is not uncommon for children this age to turn to their parents and say, "I hate you!"

## What Your Child May Be Thinking or Feeling

Just because it's dark outside, Mommy won't let me walk to my friend's house. Why won't she? I'm not afraid of the dark anymore. I'm really big now. Mommy must think I'm still afraid of the dark. She must think I'm still a baby. I know that I'm big and brave, but when Mommy won't let me leave the house when I want to, it makes me feel very small.

I'm not sure what "hate" means, but I know it's the biggest and most powerful word I know. I had to use it to show Mommy how bad I felt.

Earlier today, I used that word when my friend wouldn't let me play with his truck. I felt so bad that it made me want to not be friends. I told him I hated him and he couldn't play with any of my birthday toys. That will fix him, I'm sure.

Sometimes I feel big and strong, but at other times, I feel awful and little. When I feel little, I have to blow myself up really big so I can show other people that I'm powerful—and so I can show myself that I'm powerful.

Sometimes I feel completely overwhelmed. I don't know what to do with all the feelings I have. They spill out all over the place, so I have to fall on the floor and kick my feet and thrash my arms. Mommy calls it a temper tantrum. I don't know what that is, but I do know it feels awful to have one. It makes me feel weak and helpless.

Some people don't understand that I really don't want to have a temper tantrum. I just start feeling as though I don't know how to get what I need, and I can't keep all those feelings stuffed inside me. They come out. I'm not trying to push them out.

Everything in my life is big these days. Mommy says I'm acting dramatic, but I'm not trying to do anything special. I just have very big feelings.

## What It Means

Because four-year-olds are building a lot of power, they can become easily overwhelmed when their power is challenged. The breadth of your child's feelings during this developmental stage is enormous, ranging from supreme bossiness to helplessness. When your child feels either extreme, he is likely to react radically.

When your child says, "I hate you," all he really means is that he is angry at you. Your response should be, "I see that you're angry. Tell me why you're angry at me." Encouraging your child to express feelings directly and accurately is a critically important skill. Help your child build that skill now.

Also remember that vulnerable feelings always exist under anger. Your child feels helpless, hopeless, frustrated, or afraid. Any of these feeling hurts a lot. Anger provides a shield that protects your child.

But that anger has to be verbalized directly, not hidden behind hurtful words. You cannot dictate whether you or your child feels angry. You can set guidelines on how that anger will be expressed. That's a skill to teach your child.

If your child is temper-tantrum prone, he is likely to be accused of throwing tantrums "to get what he wants." The tantrum occurs because your child doesn't know a better way to get what he wants. Your job is to teach him better, or more acceptable, ways to express his anger.

Your child also feels overwhelmed with need, and with no satisfactory way to protect his sense of powerfulness, he "comes unglued"; hence, a tantrum results. Many adults have tantrums, too, but instead of throwing themselves on the floor kicking and screaming, they rage, physically or verbally, become hypercritical, or burst into uncontrollable tears.

These displays of emotion are also the result of feeling powerless, of lacking the ability to obtain what you need to feel good. Adults and children who have tantrums are not bad people. They are needy people who have to be given more power, not less.

Sometimes anger is displaced from its original source onto another source. For a child, the safest place to aim anger is often at a loving parent. This usually happens when your child has had a hard day in the neighborhood. Perhaps he was intimidated or taken advantage of by an older child. Or maybe his favorite toy broke. He comes into the house and starts throwing things around, or he sasses you.

Rather than jumping on your child, immediately scolding him for his behavior (though that is the most normal reaction), stop. Ignore the behavior. Instead, ask your child what's bothering him. You may say, "You seem really angry. What's going on? Use your words to tell me what is bothering you. Did something happen while you were outside?" Then be quiet. Give your child time to respond. Don't nag.

Being dramatic and having big feelings at this stage is just your child's way to protect his more-helpless feelings. Your child hasn't learned to moderate his behavior, yet. But, with your help, he will.

## What to Do

**Teach your child how to express his anger.**
No matter what form your child's anger takes, help him express his anger effectively. Have your child "use his words" to express feelings. This is an excellent way to teach your child a skill that lasts his whole life.

**Provide your child with a good model for the expression of powerfulness.**
Your behavior and words are the most powerful tools you have to teach your child, and you do teach, whether you know it or not. You are a model for your child. He tends to imitate you, so act the

way you want your child to act. Speak the way you want your child to speak. Know that this kind of learning is long-lasting and continues long after your child is grown and out of your sight.

**Use your child's flair for the dramatic.**
Since dramatic expressions of powerfulness are common at this stage, you may as well take advantage of them. Role-play using storybook characters. Assign your child a powerful role while you take the role of the underling.

Four-year-olds also enjoy a game in which they play the parent and you play the child, for a time—say, ten to thirty minutes. This role reversal tells your child that you respect him. As a bonus, you learn how your child sees you because he acts it out right in front of you.

## What Not To Do

**Do not be fooled by your child's displays of anger.**
When your child throws a temper tantrum, yells, says, "I hate you," or generally displays signs of anger, don't be fooled into thinking that he purposely tries to get away with something. Instead, realize that your child feels overwhelmed and doesn't know how to get his needs met. Instead of scolding your child, teach him.

**Do not demand that your child hide his emotions from you.**
Sometimes parents demand good behavior from their child, which means the child may not display angry feelings or behavior. Then, when the child is out of the parents' sight, the anger pours out—on everyone else. The child displaces his anger.

Since feelings don't just go away, you can be sure they brew underground. You and your child will be a lot better off if you know openly what your child feels. Then you can help your child learn appropriate ways to express his feelings. Otherwise, you fool yourself into believing that your child is good, when in reality your child is a ticking time bomb.

**Do not meet power with power.**
Don't allow yourself to come to your child's level. If your child is out of control, you must stay in control. Even though you may feel irritated or frightened by your child's behavior, take a few deep

breaths and collect your thoughts before you do anything.

I've heard parents say, "I only spank my child if I'm angry." First of all, spanking your child serves no useful purpose. It only teaches your child to be submissive to someone who is physically and emotionally stronger than he, and it teaches your child that physical violence is the way to solve problems.

Second, you are out of control if you react while you're angry. Your brain is not engaged, so you cannot make quality decisions about how to teach your child to act appropriately the next time he needs something. Your job is to think, not react as though you are also four years old.

# Five to Six and a Half Years:
## Self-Control

Around the age of five or so, your child shifts from concentrating on developing her powerfulness to focusing on being self-controlled. Up until this time, your child's behavior has either reflected a desire to gain your approval or a fear that she would get into trouble doing "the wrong thing." Your child relied on someone outside of herself to direct the way she acted.

At five, your Super Woman becomes Goody-Two-Shoes. This transformation reflects the fifth and final developmental stage: self-control. Each of the other four stages—trust, identity, competence, and power—contribute to your child's ability to reach this stage. Your child now works to acquire self-control, which means she can be counted on to behave herself even when you or another authority figure is not around.

True self-control relies on your child's ability to feel within herself the rightness or wrongness of an act. And that ability, in turn, depends upon your child's empathy, which doesn't develop prior to about age five. Empathy, the ability to feel what another person feels, comes from bonding with someone.

During the first stage of emotional development, your child establishes this bond as she learns that she can trust you to meet her needs at a time when she can't meet them herself. As she figures out her identity at age two, your child creates a self that provides her the ability to control herself from within. As she builds her sense of competence at age three, your child comes to believe in herself and in what she can do—a belief imperative for the budding self-controlled five-year-old. Finally, your child's four-year-old powerfulness fuels the previously learned skills so she can adamantly stand alone—seemingly against the whole world.

When your child develops a sense of trust that her needs will be met, when she knows who she is, when she has a sense of competence, and when she feels powerful to get her needs met in socially acceptable ways, your child automatically, at about age five, strives for self-control. Your child wants to establish control over her behavior—not because you want her to, but because she believes it is the right thing to do.

In this section, you will learn how to help your child understand, cope with, and use her newly-developed values: empathy, honesty, and fairness. You will also learn how to teach your child to handle differences and control herself, whether or not you are present. Your job will be, as before, to serve as a model with whom your child can identify, and to guide the development of your child's values and beliefs, teaching her how to handle situations in constructive ways.

As your child masters this fifth stage of development, she becomes an emotionally healthy, well-behaved child who can follow her dreams, build relationships, and act responsibly.

# Establishing Control

## Your Child's Behavior

Your five-year-old may still be fairly bossy, as bossy as he was at age four. But he may also seem to be a know-it-all in other ways.

Your child may think he always knows the right and best way to do things, even things that don't involve him in any way. You may feel that, in addition to wanting to be in charge of his own life, your child also wants to take over yours.

For example, if you are on a diet and take a low-calorie, nonfat dessert out of the freezer, your five-year-old may appear in the kitchen and tell you that the dessert is not on your diet. Even if you explain to your child that the dessert has no fat and only a few calories, he may continue to hold his ground, telling you that you shouldn't do what you're doing. You may find yourself becoming angry. After all, you're an adult. Shouldn't you have a right to eat what you'd like without a five-year-old telling you what to do?

Your child may also give a younger sibling a lesson in table manners, saying that everyone should use silverware and not slurp. His younger brother may be too young to understand such rules, as your older child was too young just a few years ago, but your five-year-old may not care about such explanations.

## What Your Child May Be Thinking or Feeling

Now that I'm five years old, I know almost everything. I'm nearly grown up. I know what is right and what is wrong. I don't mind telling Mommy or anyone else what I know. Like when Mommy was eating a dessert. She told me she was on a diet, and I know that desserts are not on diets. I told her so.

There's a new feeling inside me now. It makes me want to do what I've been taught. When my little brother picked his food up with his fingers and slurped his drink, I thought it was gross. I've been taught that is not the right way to eat. Everyone should always use a fork, even little brothers.

I felt as though I should tell him the right way to do it. So I said,

"Use your fork or don't eat!" I thought that would do the job, but he still didn't listen to me. He said he likes to use his fingers.

Doesn't anyone else in this family know how to do anything right? Do I have to teach everyone everything? When will they start listening to me?

## What It Means

When your child is five years old, many new skills emerge so strongly that they need modification to be used with balance. Self-control is one of those skills, and it may, at first, make your child appear bossy, critical, judgmental, demanding, and a know-it-all. Don't worry. Your child won't always be this way. He'll moderate these traits.

You must also remember that your child's cognitive capability is still developing. At five, your child is quite concrete in his thinking—everything is seen in terms of black and white. Something is either his way or no way. Later, your child will be able to think more abstractly and realize that the world has many gray areas, areas that are not so easily explained in totally right and wrong terms.

Your child tends to reflect the attitudes of parents and other close adults. He reflects your behavior even more than your words, so telling your child to "Do as I say, not as I do," is a waste of time and energy.

Because your child has bonded with you, he wants to be like you and he will adopt your values and try very hard to live by them—naively so. Not until adolescence will your child begin to question what he learns at this age. Many of the values learned now stay with your child the rest of his life, though he will have to rethink them to make them his own.

At five, your child begins to feel guilt when he does something other than what you want. He'll try very hard to do what he "should." Your child wants desperately to please you and other important adults, such as teachers, police, and coaches.

If a child is raised with too much fear to bond properly to the adults who care for him, the development of conscience will be slowed. Then the child will have trouble behaving on his own. Fear can come from too much strictness or control, the use of guilt-producing techniques, or physical or verbal abuse that makes or forces a child to do what grownups demand.

Such a child tends to become sneaky, hard to trust, and even violent. He doesn't empathize with others and so cannot be counted on to treat others or himself with kindness. Limited remorse for what he's done may be the result.

Teaching your child to be self-controlled takes longer and is harder than forcing your child to behave in your presence, but the long-term ramifications are well worth the time and effort. Work with your child now, and your job later will be much easier.

## What to Do

**Support your child's desire for self-control.**
When your child tries hard to be good, recognize the effort and compliment your child. Say, "You are doing a good job controlling yourself, honey. I appreciate what you're doing."

**Be as specific as possible, reinforcing behaviors you like.**
Look for opportunities to compliment specific behaviors. Say, "When you tell me the truth, I really appreciate it," or "I sure do like it when you say 'thank you.' Thank you."

**Admit when you vary from your own rules or standards.**
From time to time, all adults get off course and do something they wish they hadn't done. When this happens to you, acknowledge to your child what you have done and share how you plan to fix it. Say, "I believe in driving safely, but today I went too fast and a policeman gave me a speeding ticket. That reminded me that I must watch how fast I drive. I'm also going to take a defensive driving class to help remind me. When you drive, I bet you'll remember better than I did today."

This kind of dialogue also provides a teachable moment, which is much more effective than threatening or warning your child.

**Act the way you want your child to act.**
If you tell your child one thing but do another, your child will do what you do. That is human nature. You are a powerful model for your child's behavior. Not only will your child appreciate the gift of

values you give, but you will benefit by having a clean conscience. You'll sleep better.

## What Not to Do

**Do not worry about being perfect.**
You shouldn't worry about being perfect. No one is. Actually, admitting when you "mess up" provides a teaching opportunity that shows your child how to fix mistakes.

**Do not lie about what you do or don't do.**
On some level, children know when their parents lie. So if you err from proper behavior, say so and say why. If you don't know why, find out.

If you told a lie, tell your child. For example, say, "I told you I would take you to the park, but I can't. I have work to do. I knew I had too much work, but I told you because I didn't want to disappoint you and I wanted to do something nice with you. Next time I'll tell you the truth even though it may disappoint you."

Give your child permission to be honest, too. Your child may tell you that he's not sure he can trust you the next time you say you'll do something. Reassure your child that you've learned your lesson, but that you understand his hesitancy. Of course, you can't repeatedly make excuses, or your child will stop believing you.

**Do not use fear, force, or shame to control your child.**
The development of self-control depends on teaching your child to believe in himself and to follow the values that you have instilled in him. When you use fear, force, guilt, or shame to control your child, he continues to require someone outside of him to control his behavior. The child cannot be counted on or left to his own devices. He requires outside supervision.

Teach, don't threaten. Say, "I want you to do what your teacher asks in school, so you can learn a lot and use that good brain of yours. I know you will. I want to thank you ahead of time."

**Do not take your child's judgments or criticisms personally.**
When your child points out that you don't do something quite right, realize that he's trying to build his self-control. For awhile,

your child may be a little hard to live with, but this will pass, and he'll have gained a lot of self-control. Meanwhile, you be the judge of your own behavior.

**Do not penalize your child for being bossy, judgmental, or critical.** Rather than penalizing your child for behavior typical of this age, compliment him on trying to be self-controlled. Teach your child to be empathetic. Say, "I can see you want your brother to behave the way in which you believe is right, but I must ask you to not bother him. He's only three, and he'll learn when he's your age. Be gentle with him."

# Feeling Empathy

## Your Child's Behavior

Your five-year-old may suddenly start to "wear her heart on her sleeve," and bring home every stray animal and pet she can find. Your child may even bring friends or other children home if she thinks that they're better off at your house than at their own. Or she may start to ask for a baby brother or sister—someone she can help care for.

Your child may suddenly feel empathy for everyone and everything she sees. She may worry about the birds in the winter: How do they find food? And she may want you to go to the store especially to buy bird food so she can put it on top of the snow. Or your child may worry about the men repairing the sidewalk in front of your house: Are they thirsty? She may want you to go to the market to buy them some lunch.

## What Your Child May Be Thinking or Feeling

I love animals. I feel them in my heart. Sometimes I cry when they are hurt. I can feel what they must feel. I try very hard to help every animal I find. When they get better, it's very hard to give them away, unless someone else especially needs them. I could never just put them out on the street. They may get hungry and not have anyone to feed them, or they may get careless and get hit by a car.

People are just like animals in some ways, only bigger. So if I have a friend who isn't happy at her own house—maybe her sister is screaming at her for no reason—I like to take care of my friend by bringing her to my house.

Mommy can do anything—she can help people feel better when they have a problem. She's really nice and her hugs are great. But she can be tough if we get into trouble. I have a friend who needs big hugs but who also needs someone who can be tough. I brought her home to Mommy. I know Mommy can handle this.

I think a lot about how much I love my family. I love my family so much that I think it would be fun to have a little brother or sister.

Mommy says she doesn't think that sounds like such a good idea. Well, if I can't have one of those, maybe I'll have a possum or a parrot.

## What It Means

Part of developing self-control is the ability to feel empathy for someone or something else. Prior to age five, children do what they do because they want your approval or are afraid of your response to them. They don't yet have empathy, which is the ability to put themselves in another person's shoes—to feel what the other person feels.

Some people believe that if you don't force children to do things, control their every move, or use punishment as a means to limit their behavior, they will not be good or controlled. Ironically, just the opposite is true. The child who has experienced love, unconditional acceptance, and clear limits that are reinforced with guidance rather than punishment develops empathy and wants to behave in socially acceptable, loving, and compassionate ways. This child develops self-control.

Sensitivity to others and their feelings is a prerequisite for developing empathy. As your child learns to feel what goes on around her, she builds an information data bank about feeling. If your child receives loving feelings, supportive guidance, and instruction in how feelings work, she becomes aware of her own feelings during the second stage of her growth, as a two-year-old. Your child stays open to the people whom she trusts. She continues to accumulate information and emotional skills.

Because empathy is so important to the healthy growth of your child, you want to respond positively and supportively with sensitive guidance to help your child do what is right. Five-year-olds don't know what is right until they are taught. You teach those lessons every day through the way you live your life.

As your child cares for bugs, birds, cats, and dogs, she builds the skills needed to treat people well. Your child's awareness of how you help her transfers to her care for the critters with which she comes in contact. In the next step, your child learns to care for other children with whom she identifies. They are, after all, like her. Finally, you'll notice that your child comes to you and offers support if you have a headache. Your child mimics the way you care for her, by turning the tables to care for you.

During this fifth stage of development, your child also becomes aware of other, less fortunate, children. If you've done your teaching work, your child begins to realize that there are no bad guys, but that people who treat others poorly don't know any better, or they may feel hurt inside themselves and need help to act differently.

## What to Do

**Provide a consistent model of self-control for your child to follow.** You are the most powerful teaching model in your child's life. Your child will do exactly what you do. So act the way you want your child to act.

**Be sensitive to your child's feelings.**
When your child is hurt, upset, angry, or overwhelmed, be sure to notice and take the time to talk with her in a sensitive way. Let your child know you notice how she feels. Tell your child how to handle her feelings. Help your child figure out socially acceptable ways to feel better.

You may want to say, "Honey, you seem to be feeling angry today. Tell me what happened." When she does, try to understand what happened from her viewpoint, not yours. It will make sense to you then. If you don't understand, tell your child that, saying, "I don't understand what happened to make you so upset, but I want to help you anyway."

**Ask what would be helpful.**
What has happened to your child is less important than your support of her. Ask what she would consider helpful. You can give your child choices: "Would you like to come sit on my lap for a while? Or would you rather come in the house and have a time-out? We can talk about what happened if you like." Don't try to force talking, though, if your child isn't ready.

**Show your child how to comfort and be gentle.**
The next critter that appears in your yard or home will provide a good model for teaching your child how to compassionately take care of another. Together, you and your child can check the newcomer. Let's say a butterfly has inadvertently flown into your house. It's doomed to die if it doesn't get out. You can instruct your child to get a container to catch it. While you're catching the butterfly, you can say, "I imagine that butterfly is very afraid. It probably doesn't know where it is, and it just wants to get out. Let's be very gentle so we don't hurt it. We'll set it free. I think that will make it very happy, don't you?"

Teach your child to ask other people what would help. If your child thinks that her friend could use one of your hugs, she could ask the friend, "Would you like one of my mommy's hugs?" It's just possible that the friend doesn't want one, but maybe she'd like a cool drink of juice and the opportunity to stay over for dinner.

**Teach your child about feelings.**
Although you taught your child about feelings in the second stage of development, when her identity was developing, you must teach her again now. Your child has grown a lot cognitively and will understand her feelings on a more mature level than at an earlier age.

You can use yourself as an example. If you stub your toe, you may say to your child, "Ow! That hurts." Then, turn to your child and say, "Remember when you banged your toe? Mine hurts the same way now."

## What Not to Do

**Do not tell your child she's silly or she shouldn't feel the way she feels.**
When a child expresses her feelings, you may feel she's making a big thing out of nothing. But to the child, what happened may feel enormous. What you don't want to say is, "Don't be so silly," or "Don't be so dramatic."

Instead say, "I'm so sorry. I don't know how to fix this for you, but I understand you feel bad. It's okay to cry or be mad. Use your words to tell me how you feel. We'll figure out what to do to help you out."

**Do not treat your child as though she requires massive force to learn to behave.**
Use firmness, yes, to guide your child to act the way you want. Stop her when you don't like what she is doing. But don't use hitting, cursing, spanking, shaming, or guilt-producing language to make your child mind. Saying, "I'll show her," only proves that you are stronger; such an attitude doesn't teach self-control.

# Developing Honesty

## Your Child's Behavior

You may notice that your child lies to you more than he used to. He may play with matches, even though you told him not to, and he will deny it, even if you catch him red-handed. Your child may say he didn't eat any cookies, even though he still has crumbs on his face. Or he may say he didn't go outside, even though you clearly saw him open the door and walk out.

And your child may cheat when he plays games with his friends. For example, he may say he won fair and square, even though you saw him move the spinner so it would point to the number he needed to win.

When you try to talk to your child about this behavior, he may not look you directly in the eye. Instead, he may just hang his head and remain silent.

## What Your Child May Be Thinking or Feeling

I know so much more than I used to. I'm getting very grown up. I can even tie my shoes now. But I still have to learn about a lot of things. For example, I really wanted to learn about matches. I tried to find out how to make a fire with them once, but I couldn't do it. When Mommy caught me, she was very mad. I was scared. I couldn't even look at her. I felt so scared that I had to tell her I didn't do it.

I really don't want to tell lies, but I get scared of what will happen if I tell the truth. Sometimes I can't keep myself from doing things. I know what is right. I know I'm not supposed to sneak cookies, but I can't help myself sometimes. I'm afraid that if I ask Mommy, she'll say no. So I just go ahead and take them. But after I do, they don't even taste very good because of the bad feeling I have inside. I know I've done something wrong.

I like to play with my friends, but I have to win to feel good. I get really scared that I won't be able to win when we play. My friend is older than me, and he always wins. That makes me feel helpless. I need to win, at least sometimes. I didn't think moving the spinner would hurt much, but then I got that bad feeling in my stomach again, because I knew I did something wrong. I know I shouldn't cheat, but I want to win so bad.

## What It Means

Although many of your child's feelings are under control at this age, a new feeling is now emerging and causing trouble. Your child now has a new feeling when he acts wrongly. When you see your child look humble or penitent, you know he's learned to feel guilt.

Guilt means your child knows that some things are bad and some are good. Generally, your child now knows the difference.

Guilty feelings mean your child wants to do what is right. Guilty feelings also make your child feel anxious. These anxious, fearful feelings cause your child to lie, until he learns that telling lies makes situations worse, and telling the truth makes situations better.

Your job during this time is to make it safe for your child to tell the truth. But until your child learns about honesty, he will try different approaches to get what he needs or what he thinks he needs.

As a young five-year-old, your child experiments with honesty to see what happens. He discovers guilt and begins to learn how bad it feels. As your child progresses through the year, he begins to inhibit his actions because of guilt. Then you know your child is well on his way to developing self-control. That is fortunate indeed.

## What to Do

**Make it pay for your child to be honest with you.**
Encourage your child to tell you the truth. Say, "When you tell me the truth, I will help you get what you want. If you tell me a lie, then I'll not help you, and you will have to suffer the consequences."

If your child is a "cookie thief," you may want to say, "The next time you want a cookie, tell me. I'll try to help you find a way to have one. Or, at least, you can pick out a cookie that you can save until after you eat dinner. But if you sneak a cookie, you'll have to give it back, and tomorrow you can't have one either."

**Tell your child why you don't want him to do dangerous things.**
Instead of only telling your child not to do something, tell him *why* you don't want him to do something. Even show your child the results, if possible.

Children of five are fascinated with fire. You would do well to teach your child how to safely light matches, and let him see how matches start fires. You can do this either in a safe backyard cooking area or at a park. Show your child how wind affects the flames, and how quickly dry things catch on fire. Have water at hand for your child to douse the fire. Then tell him to ask you when he wants to light a fire, so you can do it together safely.

Make a trip to the fire station. If your child's school has not done so, you can arrange for such a visit. Firefighters are delighted to educate children about fire safety.

**Help your child find ways to sometimes win at games.**
Adults have to help equalize differing skill levels between players. Children of different ages who play together need an adjustment so the younger children don't always lose. That is too much to expect of anyone, especially a five-year-old.

One trick is to give extra points to the weakest player. (When adults do it, it's called handicapping.) If the game board has two sides, another trick is to swap sides midway through the game, so the stronger player has to take over the losing side of the board and make up the deficit.

**Explain about guilt to your child.**
The feeling of guilt is new to your child. Explain what he feels. Ask your child, "When you lit the match, what did you feel? Did you notice a different feeling?" As your child nods, ask him to point to the place in his body where he felt the feeling. Then say, "That's guilt that you felt. It happens to me, too, when I do something I'm not supposed to do. It makes me feel scared I'll get caught. It's like a warning sign that tells us we have to change what we are doing. Use it to help you feel good about yourself again."

**Be definite with your limits and repercussions.**
When your child is dishonest or does something that is dangerous

when he's been told not to, stop him and say, "I cannot let you lie to me or do dangerous things. You'll have to stay in the same room with me or with the babysitter until I can trust you to control yourself."

You may say, "If you lie to me, I can't trust you, and trusting you is the most important thing in the whole world. If you tell me the truth, I can help you. If you lie, you'll have to stay in the house with me and I won't be able to let you do what you want. I know, though, that you are learning to tell the truth, and you will soon have your freedom."

## What Not to Do

**Do not try to beat honesty into your child.**
The more you try to force your child to be honest, the more sneaky he becomes. At ages five and six, fear usually underlies dishonesty. If you use pressure techniques, you only increase your child's fear. As a result, your child shows you good behavior and goes elsewhere to let out his rage at being punished or severely treated. Although the repercussions of force may not become apparent to you for some years, sooner or later your child will sneak out the window, steal the family car, or hurt others maliciously. Neither you nor your child deserves this outcome.

**Do not lie to your child.**
The best teacher is a good model. Tell your child the truth even when he doesn't like it. If your child doesn't want to go to the baby-sitter's, don't trick him. Instead, say honestly, "I have to go to work, and you have to go to the babysitter's." Say it in a matter-of-fact way. If your child screws up his face, say, "I realize you don't want to go. You can tell me that. I will be back at 5:30 this afternoon, then let's do something you like to do."

Recognize your child's displeasure, and honestly tell him what will happen. This helps your child accept unpleasantness. Give your child some reward for accepting what is unpleasant. Remember, your child is learning how to live life, even when it's hard for him.

**Do not make your child apologize.**
While your child learns about playing fairly, don't demand he apologize. Your child has enough to cope with already. Besides, apologies are for accidents and unintentional hurts to someone else. Your child meant to cheat and is not likely to honestly feel sorry. Forcing your child to apologize for lying or cheating is, therefore, teaching him to lie.

Instead, help your child mature into playing games fairly, as his ability improves and he has a fair chance to win sometimes.

# Requiring Fairness

## Your Child's Behavior

You may find that your five-year-old uses the sentence, "It's not fair!" more than any other. Your child may use that phrase to describe anything, from the fact that it's raining when she wants to go outside to swim, to the fact that her last name begins with a "W," so she is assigned a chair at the back of the classroom. Maybe a fourth grader tricks your child into giving away her lunch money, and your child can't understand how someone can act so unfairly.

You know how unfair the world can be, and you'd like to protect your child from those feelings, but you know you can't. Your child may genuinely be treated unfairly in some circumstances, but she may use the phrase, "It's not fair!" so often that you may have trouble initially telling which are the really serious issues.

## What Your Child May Be Thinking or Feeling

I sure am big now. In fact, I'm so big that I go to school where my big sister goes. I even washed my face the first day of school without fussing because I was so excited to go. But when I got there, my teacher wasn't fair. She put my friends up at the front of the room, and I had to sit in the back.

I want to sit with my friends. I don't know anyone who sits at the back of the room. I would feel more important sitting in the front than in the back, but my teacher says I have to sit in the back because my last name starts with "W." That's not a very good reason. It's not fair.

In my family, Mommy and Daddy always tell me to tell the truth. They say that if I tell the truth, everything will be okay. I told my teacher the truth. I told her I wanted to sit at the front of the room, but she didn't care. She put me in the back anyway. That's not fair.

I feel really bad that the fourth-grade girl tricked me into giving away my lunch money. I believed her when she said she wanted to help me. I thought she was being nice to me. Now I am not only hungry, but I'm scared. Can't I trust kids at school?

If things aren't fair, then I don't know what to count on. It makes me feel helpless and powerless. I have to have some control over what I do.

## What It Means

Trying to explain fairness to your five-year-old is not an easy job. As adults know, life isn't always fair. That's more than a five-year-old can accept. The trick is to reach a balance between helping your child maintain trust and teaching her about some of the inequities and hard lessons of life.

You cannot prepare or even warn your child about everything that can hurt her or she will be afraid to go out the door. Some of the things that hurt her, such as having a name that starts with "W," are beyond your control to foresee. So, what you must do is be available to your child; let her tell you what happens to her. Then you can help your child deal with the difficulties she encounters.

Your child, at five, is at her peak of innocence; at the same time, she has a low level of experience. From here on out, your child loses some innocence as she gains experience. She also learns to assess situations more realistically. For now, though, your job is to support your child when she gets hurt or tricked. Your child will learn.

Gullibility comes from inexperience, too. Because you have done your job well, your child has a high level of trust in others. You have to begin to explain, if you haven't already, that not everyone in the world can look out for your child's best interests. Explain that some people fear not having enough for themselves, so they try to cheat other people. You can talk about how some people feel needy; explain that these people don't know how to empathize with others or take care of people who are younger or weaker.

During this period, you can explain how rules provide guidelines for behavior. You will, however, have to explain that not all rules are fair for everyone involved. You may want to suggest that your child think about ways to change the rules that seem unfair. Then you can talk about how rules get changed. That makes quite a good social studies lesson.

However, don't forget that your child's feelings are hurt. Understand and nurture those feeling before you teach the lessons.

Many a shiny apple or a walk in the park has soothed a child hurt by the unfairness of life. Soothe first, talk later.

You may want to share an experience or two from your own childhood about dealing with an unfair situation. That lets your child know that she's not the only one in the world who has suffered an inequity.

## What to Do

### Console your child.
When your innocent five-year-old feels unfairly treated, console her. Lectures and long dissertations about how life isn't fair miss the mark at this time. What your child needs is empathetic understanding and a supportive arm to soothe her bruised feelings.

### Teach your child to be less gullible.
Explain to your child that not everyone shares the same values as your family. You may say, "The fourth grader doesn't know that it is not nice to trick a kindergartner. Maybe no one taught her, or maybe someone tricked her and she took it out on you. That's not right, though."

You may want to add, "You have to be careful until you know whether a person can be trusted to treat you right. Being careful means not giving a person money, not going any place with her, and not lending her anything. Ask me or a teacher first if you don't know a person well. We'll help you learn whom to trust."

### Talk about rules and why they exist.
When your child has to constantly follow rules made by other people, she feels taken advantage of. Talk about the rules you have around the house and why you have them. For example, one rule may be, "You can't take food in your bedroom." The reason for the rule may be to prevent bugs from being drawn to leftover crumbs.

Rules have to make sense or, at least, have a rational purpose. Be honest with your child. If you've set bedtime at eight o'clock and your child complains she's not tired, tell her the truth about why bedtime is set for that hour. Maybe you chose that hour because you're tired and need some quiet time. Your child can understand the truth, and that will make her more willing to cooperate with the rules. You may decide to compromise and simply have your child go to her room at eight, without requiring her to go right to sleep.

## What Not to Do

**Do not express bitterness to your child.**
If you feel that life is unfair and that makes you bitter, don't pass your feelings on to your child. Get help for yourself. Your own inner child needs support and counseling. Otherwise, you will continue to feel bad, create hurtful situations for yourself, and pass unresolved emotions on to the next generation.

**Do not scare your child to try to protect her.**
In the name of protection, some parents teach their children not to trust anyone, ever. Don't tell your child horror stories about what happens to innocent little children; that only serves to create a very frightened child. You can teach self-protection by explaining that not everyone is as trustworthy as your family. You don't have to go into all the gory details.

Be firm, saying, "You are not to go anywhere with a stranger. If someone stops you, say, 'Daddy and Mommy won't let me.' Then immediately tell me or your teacher or one of your friend's parents what happened." Have your child repeat back your instructions. You may even want to role-play a situation or two.

**Do not let older children scapegoat or take advantage of your child.**
A five-year-old cannot protect herself against an older child. Your child needs your help. Later she will learn to take care of herself, but now she's still too young. You may wish to speak to the older child directly, saying, "I understand that you sold my daughter your lunch yesterday. You tricked her. I decided to talk with you directly so you can give her her money back and apologize. Bring it tomorrow and I'll meet you here in the hallway with my daughter. If you don't, I'll have to speak with your parents." Then do what you say.

Remember, though, that such intervention will no longer be appropriate when your child is older—and may, in fact, be harmful. Evaluate each situation as it happens, to determine the correct action to take.

**Do not tell your child she is foolish to think life should be fair.**
Although you know life is not always fair, don't tell your child she
is foolish to think it should be. Your child has to believe life is fair.
She has to feel some sense of control at a time when her experience
is limited and her living skills are just developing.

# Handling Differences

## Your Child's Behavior

You will probably notice that your child can be pretty bossy. He assumes that he knows best about everything, and he may be shocked to discover that other children also think they know best.

Your child may gang up with other children to boss around another child. While your child is bossing that child, you may hear him call that child names, tell him he's ugly, or say that his hair is the wrong color.

## What Your Child May Be Thinking or Feeling

Everyone I play with should know that I know more than they do. One of my friends actually thinks he knows more about building blocks than I do. I can't believe that!

He tried to boss me around and get me to do things his way. I didn't want to. I don't want anyone to boss me around. If I don't take control, then I feel as though everyone is running right over me. Then I feel dumb and weak, and I don't like to feel that way. Some days, I have to talk really big so I don't feel so small. I want to do so many things. I don't know much about some of them, but I have to work hard to prove that I do know some things.

Sometimes some of the kids I know gang up on one person and call that person names. If they do that to me, I have to find something to do to make myself feel big and important. I get some kids to be on my side against the other ones, then I feel pretty powerful again.

There is one boy on my street who has hair that looks really different than everyone else's. I don't like his different hair. It reminds me of how scared I feel sometimes about being different. I want to be just like everyone else. If I'm not, I'm afraid I'll get left out and the other kids will tease me. I have to act tough with the kid who has different hair. That way, no one will tease me, and I won't feel scared inside.

## What It Means

As a five-year-old, your child must do everything he can to convince himself that he is powerful enough to counter his fears: fear of being left out, fear of being different, fear of being teased, and fear of feeling inadequate.

Much is happening and changing in your child's life. He often feels out of control at the very time that he is trying to achieve internal control over his behavior. Your child often bounces between feeling helpless and acting like a power maniac. He's just trying to gain a balance, but such balances take time to achieve.

Anything or anyone who is different frightens your child. Children this age can be quite cruel to other children, especially those who have observable differences. Physical characteristics, such as height, weight, hair, or skin color, suddenly become visible to five-year-olds. Before this age, they actually didn't notice them.

Those differences make your child feel out of control. To counteract his inner feelings, your child acts in controlling and, at times, hurtful ways, especially toward those who are weaker or younger. This scapegoating serves to distract attention from your child's inadequacies. It also gives your child the illusion that he is powerful.

Your job is to stop scapegoating instantly and help your child find alternative ways to feel powerful. Teaching children that differences are wonderful rather than scary is part of what you must do. If the definition of what is acceptable or preferable is very restrictive, your job will be harder. By age five, your child will already try to fit into the "acceptable" niche.

The more you notice and enjoy differences in your family and community, the more comfortable your child will be when he confronts differences. He won't have to go through such a trying time if the adults and older child with whom he associates respect differences.

When your child is scapegoated or rejected, he feels pain. Some children never want to chance feeling that pain again, so they become perpetrators, taking their fears out on others. Although such children may look powerful, anyone who scapegoats and rejects others really feels weak inside.

Your job is to support your child's feelings when others take advantage of him, while helping him find accepting and supportive environments and people. You can't be present every time your child plays away from home, but encourage him to share what happens to him. Keep your eyes open, and don't be afraid to make alternative arrangements for your child to enjoy successful relationships during this formative period.

## What to Do

### Teach your child about differences.
Differences are only different—neither better nor worse. The sooner your child is exposed to this idea, the fewer interpersonal problems he will have. Check your family's attitude about differences to determine what your child observes at home.

You may give a minilesson in brain physiology and genetics. Point out that some people have blue eyes and some have brown. Tell your child that these characteristics run in families. Say, in a matter-of-fact tone, "The neighbors on our right all have brown eyes, brown skin, and enjoy reading. Your daddy has blue eyes, light skin, and prefers playing sports. I have black hair, red skin, and sometimes enjoy reading and sometimes enjoy playing sports. We are all different."

### Stop your child from hurting others.
Anytime you observe your child taking advantage of someone, immediately stop him and remove him from the situation. Set a limit by saying, "You may not play with other children if you treat them poorly. You may not make fun of the four-year-old."

Next, discover why your child is taking advantage. Ask yourself and your child whether he is being scapegoated, either at home or by other children. Determine whether your child is being pressured into hurting others by an older or stronger child who is using your child to do his dirty work. Finally, consider whether your child simply has to learn to handle his own fears in a more constructive way.

### Teach your child to take responsibility for his fears.
When you talk with your child, remind him that everyone has fears. You may tell him a story using his favorite animals. For example, say, "Once upon a time there was a raccoon. He had a wonder-

ful striped tail and grand whiskers. But one day two armadillos came along. They had tiny tails and wonderful coats of armor around them."

Turn to your child and ask, "Which animal is best?" Since you've chosen two animals that your child likes, he'll respond, "Well, neither is best. I like them both."

Then you can say, "Wouldn't a raccoon look funny trying to be like an armadillo? Can you imagine an armadillo with a big fluffy tail? Well, that's how people are. We are all different. How about giving the raccoon a prize for being the best raccoon he can be and giving the armadillo a prize for being the best armadillo he can be?

"Then we can give you a prize for being the best Tommy you can be, and we can give the four-year-old a prize for being the best four-year-old Jacob in our neighborhood. That way we can each be the best we can be, and we don't have to judge ourselves in relation to anyone else. We can all be different, and we can all be the best."

**Help your child learn to share power.**
When your child insists on having his own way, tell him that he must take a time-out until he can share with others. Let your child play alone for a while until he is ready to give and take during playtime.

## What Not to Do

**Do not allow others to scapegoat your child.**
If a family member scapegoats your child, step in and defend him. A five-year-old cannot be expected to defend himself against an older or stronger person. Comfort your child, but don't overdo it. Simply say, "If your big sister picks on you again, let me know immediately."

Then find out why the other family member consistently takes advantage of your child. If an older sibling is responsible, initiate family counseling right away. The older child needs help with power and control. If an adult is the guilty party, confront the person immediately and suggest that the person obtain help with his or her feelings.

**Do not tease people about their differences.**
Even friendly jesting about physical characteristics, though understood by adults as a friendly game, is misunderstood by a five-year-old. Remember, this is a critical stage of development for your child. Friendly teasing can come later.

**Do not send your child out alone to face rejection.**
Sometimes adults think that sending a child out to fight his own battles teaches him to be strong. It rarely works that way, and when it does, your child's compassion is compromised.

# Being Self-Controlled

## Your Child's Behavior

You may be surprised to find that at school, your child has a lot of self-control—even though at home she bothers her brother and sister, doesn't cooperate, complains about her chores, and yells at the top of her lungs while running at full speed.

Your child may either control herself wonderfully, or seem to be totally out of control. You may not feel that your child has any middle ground. When you speak with your child's teacher, she may find it hard to believe that the quiet, self-controlled child in her classroom is a hellion at home.

## What Your Child May Be Thinking or Feeling

I really like school. Well, actually, I liked it better when I first started and everything was new and exciting. Now I'm getting pretty used to it, and sometimes it's boring. But even if I'm bored, I know I have to behave according to the rules. If I don't, I'll get in big trouble.

I'm not sure what happens when you get sent to the principal's office, but I know I don't want to find out. I do everything Mommy and Daddy taught me so I can stay out of trouble. I can do that now for a little while. I can't be on good behavior all day, but I know I can keep it up long enough to make it through the school day.

By the time I get home after school, I feel as though I have to run around, make a lot of noise, and do something to let out the tight feelings I stuffed inside all day.

When I see my brother and sister after school, I suddenly feel as though someone uncorked me. I run and yell and act crazy and bother them. They do the same with me. We love it!

Mommy tells us she gets really tired of us running around and making so much noise, but we love to wrestle and play. Sometimes Mommy yells at us and sends us to our rooms. Sometimes that helps me be quiet, but some days I can't be quiet at all.

No matter how loud I get, I know that Mommy and Daddy still love me. I'm glad.

## What It Means

Your five-year-old is learning to control herself; that means she must practice keeping her desires and feelings inside. She can only do it for a limited period of time, so your child keeps control in environments in which she feels the least safe. That may be the opposite of what you would expect.

If your child feels safe, secure, and unafraid of you, she shows you her worst behavior. I don't mean ugly, hurtful, malicious behavior, but rather the rinky-dinky behavior that is normal in childhood. Running around the house, yelling, and complaining about doing chores all fall in this category.

Siblings often pick on one another, engaging in the noisiest wrestling matches imaginable. From another room, you may think that one is killing the other. Generally, these fights are the result of children letting off steam in a safe way.

Often siblings view each other as their best play toy. Of course, one child must not consistently take advantage of another. Watch to see whether the children take turns starting the frenzy. Pay particular attention when younger children set up older siblings to get caught. Also, little girls often goad brothers into being very loud. Although the girl starts the fuss, the boy gets caught.

If your children engage in normal sibling rivalry, the best thing to do is ignore it. Tell the children you aren't going to take sides. Remember, you've already established that one is not taking undue advantage of the other. If the noise gets too loud and the children won't/can't settle down, send them to separate rooms to quiet down. Let them come out when they feel they can control themselves. If they get going again, separate them for as long as needed, which may be for the night.

Another way to teach your child self-control is to let her take pride in what is special to her. When your child is in a special environment, she controls herself because she doesn't want to damage anything. So notice in which situations your child demonstrates self-control. The more your child wants to control herself, the more practice she gets at actually doing it.

The best way to reinforce self-controlled behavior is to instill a sense of self-pride in your child. Provide your child with tangible evidence of her accomplishments. You may want to keep a chart that lists all the things your child has done that required even a little bit of self-control. Or maybe you want to note how well she treats a friend, so you glow with pride and bring your child's attention to her accomplishment.

Although your shouldn't overdo the pride thing (bumper stickers are a good example of going too far), do try your best to give your child a sense of self-pride. Don't confuse self-pride with arrogance or pridefulness. Rather, self-pride reflects the joy of being your best. It won't "spoil" your child. Self-pride is good for kids, and it's also good for adults; it's a healthy, positive way to achieve self-control.

Because you are a powerful model for your child, you and other family members should share things that you've done or problems that you've overcome that make you feel proud. Share with your children stories of overcoming handicaps, errors, or difficult habits. That way, children realize that adults are not perfect but that they work to correct what is undesirable. This effort puts the adult in charge of herself. That's exactly what you want your child to do—become self-responsible and self-controlled.

## What to Do

**Congratulate your child on her behavior.**
When a teacher or another person speaks positively about your child's behavior, say, "Thank you. I appreciate you letting me know." Then in private tell your child, "I appreciate you controlling yourself at school. You are doing a fine job being a responsible person. Thank you."

**Tell your child how you count on her.**
Before your child goes out the door, tell her how glad you are that you can count on her. "I know I can count on you to stay in control when you ride with Rob's mother. I appreciate you helping her out." This serves as a gentle reminder for your child to stay in control. It's a lot more effective than threatening, "You'd better behave yourself."

You are better off privately telling your child what you expect. You can whisper your thoughts in her ear. Your child will appreciate the privacy and like the special attention. She's more likely to try to accommodate your request under these conditions.

## What Not to Do

**Do not expect your child to be perfect.**
Your child cannot learn self-control if she never makes mistakes (which, by the way, is not possible). By identifying and taking responsibility for mistakes, your child gains self-control. Cherish your child's misbehaviors as learning opportunities while you guide your child to correct what she did wrong.

**Do not use the words "good behavior."**
Whenever possible, don't judge your child's behavior. Instead, tell your child what you do and don't like. You may say, "I like it when your teacher tells me you help out in class by not talking." This specifies that you, personally, like what your child is doing, and it tells her exactly what you like about her behavior.

Often the words "good behavior" are used without defining the ingredients of good behavior to the child. Adults assume the child knows what is expected of her, but often a child has no idea what is wanted from her.

**Do not take your child's raucous behavior at home personally.**
When your child acts up at home, realize that she is letting down her guard, discharging the stress that she has accumulated during the day away from home. Although you may not particularly like the behavior that your child exhibits at home, you can understand why it is present. Limit such behavior, but don't think you did something wrong or that the behavior is against you.

Don't say, "Why don't you act as nice at home as you do in school?" That invites your child to act more poorly in school and to feel guilty at home. Neither is constructive.

**Do not shame your child for losing control.**
Under no circumstances should you use shame to try to control an errant child. To say, "Shame on you," or "How could you do such a thing?" is mean and hurtful to a child. Remember, unacceptable behavior only means that your child has not learned a better way to get what she needs.

Sometimes adults think they've taught a child how to behave, when all they've done is tell a child what they expect. That's not teaching, that's telling. You won't know if a child has learned how to behave until she can produce appropriate behavior. Refine your teaching if your child misbehaves.

# Behaving "Too Good"

## Your Child's Behavior

At about age five, your child may become something of a perfectionist. At school, he may not have time to finish his work because he spends so much time trying to do it perfectly. He may labor over his letters and numbers, and be meticulous about his artwork.

If your child helps you with a chore at home, you may notice that he needs a long time to complete the task because he tries so hard to do it perfectly every step of the way. If your child is sick, he may apologize because he doesn't want to create any additional work for you.

In general, your child may seem more like a small grownup than a child. Even at home, he may be well behaved. Your child may rarely let down his guard and go crazy.

## What Your Child May Be Thinking or Feeling

I like to get everything just right. It bothers me a lot when things are sloppy and out of order. When toys are left on my bedroom floor or clothes are left out, I feel out of control. I hate it when my brother comes in and messes up everything. I have a place for everything, and I know exactly where to find something when I want it. After my brother's been in my room, I can't find anything. I love my brother, but I don't want him in my room.

I love school. I just wish I had more time. Sometimes I feel rushed. My teacher tells me not to worry about getting everything perfect. She says I do a good job all the time, but she must understand that I don't feel good when I don't take the time to do a good job. That makes my stomach hurt.

I don't like to ask for help. I know what to do to help myself, and I like that. It makes me feel safe and secure. I know that Mommy doesn't mind helping me, but I'd rather take care of myself. That helps me to feel in control of everything.

## What It Means

Some children are neurobiochemically wired to see imperfections in their environment and in their work. Perfectionistic by nature, these children must work in an orderly manner, making certain that everything fits the model they have in mind.

When your child is constructed this way, don't worry, but also don't be seduced into thinking that your child is especially good. Your child is simply what he is: not good or bad, but just what he is. However, many people will bring many pressures to bear on you and your child. Your child is likely to be unduly rewarded for being perfectionistic.

Adults tend to like a child who acts more like a grownup than a child. So when your child acts in a mature way, you and he are congratulated. That reinforces your child to work even harder to be like a grownup. The problem is that your child must be a child to fully develop in a balanced fashion. Children should not grow up too fast, or they lose touch with the ability to relax, have fun, let down their guard, and generally enjoy the process of living.

Although you don't want to scold your child for being perfectionistic, you must provide lots of opportunities for your child to relax. Make a distinction between work and playtime, and try to find play activities that don't have to be done perfectly.

Occasionally, a child who acts like a little adult does so because he is afraid to relax. The cause of this type of perfectionism is quite different from the one described above. Rather than being born with neurobiochemical wiring that demands order, this child learns he's only safe when he keeps absolute control.

This type of child must be encouraged to relax and must be given help to feel safe enough to be a child. Sometimes you must give the youngster permission. But this must be done carefully; the extra control was locked in place for a reason. Often, this type of child comes from an environment where it's not safe to be anything less than perfect. In that case, giving the child permission to let down his guard is not a good idea, because the child may be vulnerable to punishment or disapproval at home.

But most of the time, the "too good" child doesn't demonstrate a problem or symptom. Instead, he just likes order—it's the way his mind is put together. If this description fits your child, he needs your support and assistance to balance his natural tendencies and stay in healthy control of himself.

Most children have to learn to control themselves better in order to be in control. Your child must learn to control himself less in order to be in control.

## What to Do

**Enjoy your child the way he is.**
Your job as a parent is to accept your child the way he is constructed. If your child is perfectionistic, that is fine. If your child is sloppy, that is fine, too. However, each child needs encouragement to learn balance. Your perfectionistic child must be able to do things imperfectly. Don't pressure your child, but do give him permission to allow variation.

**Help your child learn various ways to get a job done.**
Give your child a variety of opportunities to work with people who honor personal differences and skills. You may give your child a job that requires neatness and precision. For example, he may be assigned to stack the layers of lasagna in the pan. His brother may be asked to add spaghetti sauce, toss items in a pan, and stir. And you may act as the go-between so the two stay out of each other's way.

When the job is done you can say, "It took both of you with your special talents to make the lasagna." Congratulate each child on his special contribution. Then add, "Making lasagna takes two sets of skills. Working as a team got the job done."

**Give your child opportunities to relax his maturity.**
Make your perfectionistic child's assignments a little smaller so he doesn't have so much to do. You may even want to limit how much time your child spends on a project. Then insist that he do something he finds fun. But don't be surprised if what your child thinks of as fun seems like a chore to you. Honor your child's differences.

## What Not to Do

**Do not get caught in the "good child" trap.**
Culturally, children who behave maturely are considered better than children who act childishly. These mature children are called good. If you let yourself get caught in believing this, you short-change your child. He needs his childhood, so he can thrive and grow in a balanced fashion.

**Do not force your child to cut loose.**
Sometimes parents misguidedly think their child needs to loosen up, so they force their child to smear finger paints, get dirty, and act like other, less-inhibited children. That is a mistake. Don't pressure your child to be different than he is. Encourage him, sure, but don't pressure him.

You may ask the child who doesn't like to make soupy mud pies, "Would you like to help build a castle using clay tools to model the sand?" This allows your child to enjoy a social and creative activity without getting dirty.

**Do not worry that you have done anything wrong.**
More than likely, your perfectionistic child has a perfectionistic parent. So your child's perfectionism is either the result of genes or of watching and imitating a parent. Encourage open communication about how each parent is different from the other. Avoid judging one another.

**Do not overload a highly responsible child.**
Often a child who appears highly responsible and adult-like is given too much responsibility. Although the child may succeed, inside he is likely to feel inadequate.

Typically, such a child may be put in charge of a younger sibling. Not only does the older child miss out on playing in his own way, he is given responsibility that belongs to an adult. The child loses his freedom, and if anything goes wrong, he carries the guilt for years.

**Do not try to change your child into something he is not.**
If you recognize and honor a wide variation of differences between children, you will be fine with any type of child. But if you don't,

you may try to change your child into something he is not. Please don't do that.

You wouldn't consider trying to make a fish fly and breath air. Leave that to the birds. Let a fish be a fish and stay in the water. So, too, let your child be who he is.

# Experimenting

## Your Child's Behavior

Your child may experiment with words, and you may not approve of
them all. If she has a friend over, you may hear them giggle as they
use bathroom words. Or if your child is angry at someone, she may
make up a complicated name to call that person. It may be a name
that embarrasses you or one of which you don't approve.

If you don't use such words at home, your child's use of them may
really surprise you. If you do sometimes use those words against your
better judgment, your five-year-old may choose this age to mimic
them.

You may also find that your child does some things that are
clearly not allowed in your home. For example, she may go in the
garage and take out her father's tools, even though she has been
told never to touch them without permission. Or, she may climb on
the dresser and take down one of her older brother's model air-
planes—something she's been told never to do.

## What Your Child May Be Thinking or Feeling

I had to take Daddy's hammer and lumber out of the garage today.
My friend told me to get them so we could build a fort. My friend is
three years older than me, and I like to play with her. But if I don't
do what she tells me, she says I'm a baby and she won't play with
me if I am no fun.

I know I'm not supposed to take anything out of the garage without asking Mommy or Daddy. I feel bad when I do something they
said not to do. But I also feel bad when my friend won't play with me.

I felt that feeling in the pit of my stomach, the feeling Mommy
calls guilt. I didn't know how to choose between Daddy and
Mommy being mad at me and feeling lonely because my friend
wouldn't play with me.

Later, I played with a friend my own age and we had fun in my
room saying all those great words we're not supposed to say. We
love to do that, but only in private. When Mommy came in the

room, I felt that awful feeling again, right in the pit of my stomach. I hate that feeling.

It's hard to be five years old. I want to do what my parents want me to do, but I also want to do some of the things I'm not supposed to do. I don't like to feel guilty.

Why do I have to feel this way?

## What It Means

The fifth, and final, developmental stage culminates in the emergence of true self-control. That means your child learns to control her behavior whether or not you are around. You will notice the appearance of your child's conscience at this time. That conscience makes your child feel guilty when she does something that she's been taught not to do.

Remember, the empathy your child feels in relation to you is what creates her conscience in the first place. Your child wants your approval. She wants to be like you, so she mimics what you do and say. You're her model.

When your child goes against what you want, the guilty feelings march in to remind her that she's off track. Simultaneously, your child is tempted by many perfectly normal desires to act in a way that may not meet with your approval.

So, sometimes, your five-year-old is very torn between wanting to please you and wanting to do something she desires. Truly torn, your child suffers enormously. Please don't forget that. Your child is trying to sort out the toughest choices a person can make—and she is only five years old.

Rather than use force and shame to shape the behavior you see, help your child to think for herself, to listen to her feelings, and to behave in socially acceptable ways. Your guidance is necessary at this time. Before you can guide your child, however, you must be able to make good choices based on your own self-control. You must get what you need, but not at anyone else's expense. Your child models your behavior.

The use of bathroom words is a good example. Children of this age are fascinated with the process of elimination and seem to pass all the various words known to mankind to describe this function from one child to the next. Because this behavior is not shared by adults, your child becomes giggly and silly whenever she uses the words.

That's different from your child using swear words that she learns from you or other adults. Even if you don't swear, by this age your child hears older children and other adults cuss. Swear words generally give emphasis to what a person says. They provide a feeling of power at times of vulnerability. Your child quickly learns the function of such words and uses them to make the same emphasis.

However, initially, your youngster may have no idea what the words actually mean. Unlike an adult who understands their meaning, a child of five is drawn to the emotion of the words. That is what she copies.

The trick to controlling language use is to model appropriate language and to clearly set limits by saying, "I don't want you to swear. You can let off steam in other ways." The more fuss you make about the use of swear words, the more you reinforce their use. Remember, these words provide power to the speaker. Fussing about them gives them even more power.

## What to Do

### Teach your child about making hard choices.
Encourage your child to come to you when she is tempted to do something you don't want her to do; teach your child to make the tough choices in life. Say, "When you want to do something that you know is not right, please come to me so I can help you find a way to get what you want without misbehaving. I'll help you find a way."

Then praise your child for being mature enough to tackle such a hard job. You may say, "I know it's hard to make choices sometimes, especially if you feel you can't have something you feel you really need, but you're getting grown-up enough to do this."

### Teach your child how to deal with people who want her to do wrong.
By the time your child is five, you have to talk to her about people who try to get her to do things she's been taught not to do. Whether the bad influence is a child or another adult, it's time for your innocent child to take control of her actions. Your child built

power during the last stage of her emotional development; now you can help her draw upon that power to do what's right.

Tell your child, "Sometimes other kids will try to get you to do something that you know I don't want you to do. You can tell them no, or you can tell them that your daddy or mommy won't let you." Then add, "Sometimes you'll really want to do what you know you aren't supposed to do, like when your friend wanted you to get tools. That's a hard choice, but you must tell your friend, 'No, I'm not allowed to do that.' If your friend threatens to leave, or if she calls you names, just shrug your shoulders and walk away. Real friends don't act that way."

**Help your child understand the feelings that motivate her misdeeds.**
Part of your job is to teach your child about the feelings that motivate her actions. Teach your child by saying, "When you were afraid to tell your friend no because you didn't want to be lonely, you should have come to me so we could have figured out another way for you not to be lonely. You don't have to do wrong to have company."

This lesson is one of the most important lessons you can teach your child.

**Admit to doing wrong yourself.**
When you do something that makes you feel guilty, admit it, first to yourself, and then to your child. If you swear when you drop something on your toe, you can say, "I apologize for swearing. I must find a better way to let off steam when I'm hurt."

If you eat cake when you commit to a diet, say to your child, "You know, I ate cake today. I feel guilty. I've also been thinking about why I did that, since I'm trying to lose weight. I discovered that I really needed something to make me feel good, such as a big hug. No one was around, so I ate the cake to make me feel good, but that's not what cake is supposed to do. Food gives us physical energy and it is not a substitute for affection or nurturing. I will work to remember that the next time I'm tempted to eat cake while on a diet."

## What Not to Do

**Do not punish your child for being in conflict.**
When your child is coerced or tempted to go against the values you have taught, help her understand how to resolve such situations. Punishment for erring does nothing to help your child become a self-controlled person.

**Do not tell your child to do one thing while you do another.**
Always remember that you are your child's most powerful teacher; what you do is what your child learns first, retains the longest, and keeps throughout adulthood. That's a heavy burden, because it demands that you walk your talk.

**Do not call your child ugly or demeaning names.**
How you address your child is how your child comes to think of herself. You don't ever want to label your child in an insulting way. Insulting your child doesn't accomplish your goal and seriously damages your child. Call your child names that reflect what you want your child to become. You may wish to say, "You're smart. I can count on you to make good decisions. Let's talk about what happened and try to figure out a better way for next time," instead of, "You're stupid. Look at what you did."

When you appreciate your child, you nurture and teach a person of whom you can be proud. You also can be proud of your parenting job.

# Parting Remarks

Enjoy your child. Together you make a terrific team. Sure, some days are tougher than others, making parenting feel difficult. You may wonder whether you are doing anything right. Or you may be concerned that something terrible is wrong with your child. In most cases, what you experience is a normal and natural part of living with a growing child.

The best way to ensure you enjoy your child is to keep in step with your child's developmental needs. When you understand those needs, you know what to do. When you fight those needs, you feel aggravated and you slow or damage your child's growth. When you take the time to learn about your child's changing needs, you work with, not against, your child.

As generation after generation passed down the lack of understanding of the developmental stages, we learned to be out of step with our childhood needs. Don't blame your parents or yourself. They did the best they could, just as you are doing the best you can for your child.

But now you know better. You can break the cycle of nonresponsible parenting. The world will be a better place because you understood your growing child, and your child will thank you.

# Assessment Checklist for Preschoolers

## Stages of Emotional Development (Check Yes or No)

**Trust:** Does the child feel safe and secure? **Yes** **No**

- Child makes eye to eye contact. ✓ ___  ___
- Child comes to an adult and asks for help, or otherwise communicates a need for help. ✓ ___  ___
- Child can form an attachment to a caregiver other than mother. For example, the child seeks out the caregiver and misses the caregiver when not present. ___  ✓ ___
- Child shows as much interest in people as in things and activities. ___  ✓ ___
- Child is able to seek comfort from people, as well as from things (blanket, pacifier). ✗✓ ___  ___
- Child can give away a prized possession to another person (who promises to take care of it). ___  ✓ ___

**Self-Awareness:** Has the child developed self-awareness and individuality? **Yes** **No**

- Child uses such words as "mine," "me," and "I" when referring to him or herself. ✓ ___  ___
- Child knows body parts:
  eyes ✓ ___  ___
  ears ✓ ___  ___
  nose ✓ ___  ___
  how many others? _all_
- Child want to do things separately from the teacher. ✓ ___  ___
- Child has individual interests and tastes, different than other children's in the class. ✓ ___  ___
- Child can verbalize dislike for what the teacher is doing. ✓ ___  ___
- Child is aware of his or her sex. ✓ ___  ⋈
- Child can express body needs, such hunger, thirst, and the need to go potty. ✓ ___  ___

**Competence:** Does the child feel as though he or she can do things? | **Yes** | **No**

- Child verbalizes "I can do," "I do it," or "Let me do it." ✓ ____ ____
- Child "shows off" self or work, saying, "Look" or "Look at what I did." ✓ ____ ____
- Child "smugly glows" or takes pride in his or her work. ✓ ____ ____
- Child is willing to try new activities. ✓ ____ ____
- Child says "I can" frequently. ✓ ____ ____
- Child tries a difficult task several times before giving up. ✓ ____ ____
- Child realizes that although he or she can't perform a task now, he or she will be able to accomplish that task when older, rather than feeling like a failure. ✓ ____ ____

**Powerfulness:** Has the child developed a sense of powerfulness? Is the child beginning to learn the limits of that powerfulness? | **Yes** | **No**

- Child speaks and acts assertively (knows what he or she wants, and lets you know clearly). ✓ ____ ____
- Child likes to be boss at times. ✓ ____ ____
- Child can imitate right and wrong behavior, but does not yet feel what is right and wrong. ✓ ____ ____
- Child defies grownups at times. ✓ ____ ____
- Child can wait for a short while to get what he or she wants. ✓ ____ ____
- Child sometimes demonstrates impulse control, with help. ✓ ____ ____

**Self-Control:** Can the child demonstrate self-control because he or she believes that it is the right thing to do? | **Yes** | **No**

- Child knows what is right and wrong. ✓ ____ ____
- Child feels what is right and wrong. ✓ ____ ____
- Child want to do what is right. ✓ ____ ____
- Child can empathize with other people and with animals. ✓ ____ ____
- Child sometimes demonstrates impulse control when left without supervision. You can leave your child alone without the child getting into things. ✓ ____ ____
- The child feels guilty after doing something wrong. ✓ ____ ____

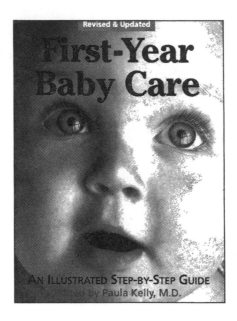

## First-Year Baby Care

Revised and Updated Edition

*Edited by Paula Kelly, M.D.*

One of the leading baby care books is now totally revised with
the most up-to-date medical facts and all new illustrations.
Key updates include the latest newborn screening and
immunization schedules, new breastfeeding information for
working mothers, expanded information on daycare options,
updated reference guides to common illnesses, and an update
on environmental and safety tips.

**Order #1119   $9.00**

## Baby & Child Emergency First-Aid Handbook

*Edited by Mitchell J. Einzig, M.D.*

"This authoritative book is the answer to every parent's fearful question: Will I know what to do if my child has a medical emergency? Concise, easily understood, and clearly illustrated instructions in large print show and tell, step-by-step, what to do and how to do it."

—Morris Green, M.D.
Professor of Pediatrics, Indiana School of Medicine

**Order #1380   $15.00**

## Baby & Child Medical Care

Revised and Updated Edition
*Edited by Terril H. Hart, M.D.*

Every first-aid or medical problem your child suffers from seems like an emergency. Newly revised and updated, this book provides illustrated step-by-step instructions that show you what to do and tell you when to call your doctor. Its visual approach makes this book much easier to use than Dr. Spock's.

**Order #1159   $9.00**

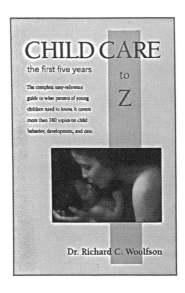

## Child Care A to Z

*by Dr. Richard C. Woolfson*

This easy-to-understand reference contains up-to-date information on 170 topics that every parent needs to know. It is organized alphabetically to help you find answers to questions about your child's physical, emotional, and intellectual development. Dr. Woolfson is known as the Dr. Spock of the United Kingdom, and his child-care experience is now available to American parents.

**Order #1010 $11.00**

# Feed Me! I'm Yours
## Revised and Expanded Edition
*by Vicki Lansky*

America's #1 cookbook for new parents contains more than 200 recipes that cover everything a parent needs to know about making homemade baby foods, teething foods, nutritious snacks, and quick, pleasing lunches. This comb-bound edition lies flat when opened.

**Order #1109  $9.00**

# Practical Parenting Tips
*by Vicki Lansky*

Here's the #1-selling collection of helpful hints for parents with babies and small children. It contains 1,001 parent-tested tips for dealing with diaper rash, nighttime crying, toilet training, temper tantrums, and traveling with tots. It will help you save time, trouble, and money.

**Order #1180  $8.00**

## Gentle Discipline

*by Dawn Lighter*

Dawn Lighter has written a breakthrough book that will change the way parents think about and practice "discipline." Most parents think of discipline as something to do after children misbehave. Lighter's book provides 50 simple, effective ways to teach children good behavior—so they won't misbehave.

**Order #1085   $6.00**

## Discipline without Shouting or Spanking

*by Jerry Wyckoff, Ph.D. and Barbara C. Unell*

Do you know all the theories about child rearing but still have trouble coping with some of your child's misbehavior? You'll love this book! It covers the 30 most common forms of misbehavior from whining to throwing temper tantrums. You'll find clear, practical advice on what to do, what not to do, and how to prevent each problem from recurring.

**Order #1079   $6.00**

# The Joy of Parenthood

*by Jan Blaustone*

This book contains hundreds of warm and inspirational "nuggets" of wisdom to help prepare parents for the pleasures and challenges ahead. Throughout the book, 24 touching black-and-white photos help convey the joy of parenthood and make this a delightful book to give or receive.

**Order #3500  $7.00**

# Familiarity Breeds Children

*Selected by Bruce Lansky*

Lansky has created a humor book for parents that will delight and revive them. This collection is a treasury of the most outrageous and clever things ever said about raising children by world-class comedians and humorists, including Roseanne, Erma Bombeck, Bill Cosby, Dave Barry, Mark Twain, Fran Lebowitz, and others. Filled with entertaining photographs, it makes the perfect gift for any parents you know—including yourself. Originally entitled *The Funny Side of Parenthood*.

**Order #4015  $7.00**

# Order Form

| Qty. | Title | Author | Order No. | Unit Cost (U.S. $) | Total |
|------|-------|--------|-----------|--------------------|-------|
| | Baby & Child Emergency First Aid | Einzig, M. | 1380 | $15.00 | |
| | Baby & Child Medical Care | Hart, T. | 1159 | $9.00 | |
| | Baby Journal | Bennett, M. | 3172 | $10.00 | |
| | Baby Name Personality Survey | Lansky/Sinrod | 1270 | $8.00 | |
| | Best Baby Shower Book | Cooke, C. | 1239 | $7.00 | |
| | Child Care A to Z | Woolfson, R. | 1010 | $11.00 | |
| | Discipline without Shouting or Spanking | Wyckoff/Unell | 1079 | $6.00 | |
| | Eating Expectantly | Swinney, B. | 1135 | $12.00 | |
| | Familiarity Breeds Children | Lansky, B. | 4015 | $7.00 | |
| | Feed Me! I'm Yours | Lansky, V. | 1109 | $9.00 | |
| | First-Year Baby Care | Kelly, P. | 1119 | $9.00 | |
| | Gentle Discipline | Lighter, D. | 1085 | $6.00 | |
| | Getting Organized for Your New Baby | Bard, M. | 1229 | $9.00 | |
| | Grandma Knows Best | McBride, M. | 4009 | $7.00 | |
| | How to Read Your Child Like a Book | Weiss, L. | 1145 | $8.00 | |
| | Joy of Parenthood | Blaustone, J. | 3500 | $7.00 | |
| | Maternal Journal | Bennett, M. | 3171 | $10.00 | |
| | Practical Parenting Tips | Lansky, V. | 1180 | $8.00 | |
| | Pregnancy, Childbirth, and the Newborn | Simkin/Whalley/Keppler | 1169 | $12.00 | |
| | Very Best Baby Name Book | Lansky, B. | 1030 | $8.00 | |
| | | | | Subtotal | |
| | | | | Shipping and Handling (see below) | |
| | | | | MN residents add 6.5% sales tax | |
| | | | | **Total** | |

**YES!** Please send me the books indicated above. Add $2.00 shipping and handling for the first book and 50¢ for each additional book. Add $2.50 to total for books shipped to Canada. Overseas postage will be billed. Allow up to four weeks for delivery. Send check or money order payable to Meadowbrook Press. No cash or C.O.D.'s, please. Prices subject to change without notice. **Quantity discounts available upon request.**

## Send book(s) to:

Name _____

Address _____

City _____ State _____ Zip _____

Telephone (_____) _____

Purchase order number (if necessary) _____

## Payment via:

☐ Check or money order payable to Meadowbrook Press (No cash or C.O.D.'s, please.) Amount enclosed $ _____

☐ Visa (for orders over $10.00 only)    ☐ MasterCard (for orders over $10.00 only)

Account #_____

Signature _____ Exp. Date_____

A **FREE** Meadowbrook catalog is available upon request.
You can also phone us for orders of $10.00 or more at 1-800-338-2232.

**Mail to:** Meadowbrook Press
5451 Smetana Drive, Minnetonka, MN 55343
Phone (612) 930-1100    Toll-Free 1-800-338-2232    Fax (612) 930-1940